AMERICA
IN THE
1980s

Timely Reports to Keep
Journalists, Scholars and the Public
Abreast of Developing Issues, Events and Trends

Published by Congressional Quarterly Inc.
1414 22nd Street, N.W.
Washington, D.C. 20037

About the Cover

The cover was designed by Art Director Richard Pottern.

Editor, Hoyt Gimlin
Associate Editor, Sandra Stencel
Editorial Assistants, Elizabeth Creel, Diane Huffman,
Production Manager, I. D. Fuller
Assistant Production Manager, Maceo Mayo

Library of Congress Cataloging in Publication Data

Editorial research reports on America in the 1980s.

Bibliography: p.

Includes index.

1. United States — Economic conditions — 1971-   2. United States — Social conditions — 1960- I. Editorial Research reports. II. Title: America in the 1980s.
HC106.7.E344   330.973'092   79-25320
ISBN 0-87187-194-7

Contents

Foreword

Rarely is the sweep of history so tidy it can be marked off neatly into 10-year intervals. But modern man, attuned to clock and calendar, seems to yearn for a periodic accounting of things. So the impulse for stock-taking and prophecy becomes irresistible at the close of one decade and the beginning of another. This may be especially true for Americans, with their bent for introspection on a national scale.

Not unexpectedly, much of the change-of-decade analysis has had to do with the national spirit, which many have examined and found wanting. When the Russian exile Alexander Solzhenitsyn spoke to the 1978 Harvard graduating class of an "intellectual malaise" in the West, there were listeners who not only accepted his judgment but thought it applied especially to the United States, his host country. A year later, in an echo of that thought, President Carter told the nation it faced a crisis of confidence, in which "our problem" was spiritual rather than material. America needed the will to do what it was capable of doing — specifically to surmount the energy crisis but more broadly to find its way once again.

Nothing contributed more to the sinking spirit of which Carter spoke than Vietnam, whose legacy is explored in one of the Reports in this book. However, some believe the "Vietnam syndrome" is being shedded at last. The catalyst for this change was the shock of seeing American taken hostage in Iran. George Ball is one who thinks the Iranian drama moved the country to overcome its guilt about Vietnam. Ball speaks with the authority of a former Under Secretary of State who earned the reputation as the chief in-house dissenter to the government's Vietnam war policy.

If Americans have cast off some of their psychic burdens upon entering the 1980s, they continue to be haunted by other problems of the past. The debilitating effect of inflation on families and the related energy shortages were added in the 1970s to concerns for the environment, questions of racial fairness in the job market, and what some perceive as America's waning work ethic. These troubling concerns, carrying over into the new decade, are examined in the various Reports making up this book. We hope they will aid our understanding as the 1980s unfold.

Hoyt Gimlin
Editor

Washington, D.C.
January 1980

AMERICA IN THE 1980s

by

William V. Thomas

Nov. 30
1 9 7 9

AMERICA IN THE 1980s

"IT IS EASY to see the beginning of things, and harder to see the end," author Joan Didion wrote toward the close of the previous decade. The ambiguities of the future, she observed, often appear more attractive and in some ways more manageable than "the broken resolves" of the past.[1] Perhaps it is the urge to look back, to see where we went wrong, that gives us pause each passing decade. Perhaps it is the peculiar American devotion to new starts. In any case, however arbitrary its divisions, the calendar does impose certain milestones on our experience both as individuals and as a nation. And as decades change, it is the perspective from these vantage points we are inclined to study with greater urgency and purpose, if only to locate where we think we are.

At the close of the eighth decade of the 20th century, Americans seem confronted by a crisis of confidence. Ten years ago, it was the war in Vietnam that tried the nation's moral sense. Today, there is what some have called "a war with ourselves." In his address to the nation on the energy shortage last July 15, President Carter said "our problem" is spiritual, not material, that it arose from a disenchantment with modern affluence and the gospel of plenty.

Echoing Alexander Solzhenitsyn's attack on the "intellectual malaise" of the West a year earlier at the Harvard commencement,[2] Carter said: "We have discovered that owning things and consuming things does not satisfy our longing for meaning. We have learned that piling up material goods cannot fill the emptiness of lives which have no confidence or purpose." For the first time in this country's history, he added, "a majority of our people believe that the next five years will be worse than the past five years. . . ."

Although Carter pronounced the American Dream in critical condition, others say his comments did not reflect the attitude of millions of people who are content with their lives and their future prospects. There is a great number of ordinary citizens who hold a view "fundamentally different from the president's portrait of distress and decline," wrote Robert G. Kaiser and Jon Lowell, authors of *Great American Dreams* (1979). In a

---

[1] Joan Didion, *Slouching Towards Bethlehem* (1968).

[2] For the text and background of the Russian exile's speech, see *Historic Documents of 1978*, Congressional Quarterly Inc., pp. 403-417.

society whose "truck drivers can earn more money than bank presidents, whose coal miner's wages exceed $20,000 a year, the traditional social categories no longer make sense. . . ."

We have created a two-car, boat-in-the-garage, cabin-at-the-lake class that defies old measures of social rank [they wrote]. These Americans define the popular culture of our time. Their preferences produced urban sprawl, highway culture, and the decay of the old central cities. They sustain the mania for sports, fast food chains, Ford and GM. They made millionaires of the makers of CB radios and striped tennis sneakers. To a degree that may be unfashionable to acknowledge, these Americans seem to be having a hell of a time.[3]

The children of the so-called "permissive generation" of the late 1940s and 1950s became the adults of the "acquisitive generation." *Time* magazine described them as "part of the instant-gratification, self-indulgent 'Me Decade,' with a taste for high-priced living and little interest in self-denial."[4] If the shared characteristic of this new privileged class is its optimistic intensity, suggested political commentator Richard Reeves, its weakness is its "retreat into individualism."[5] America emerging from the 1970s, according to one sober assessment, "is a nation aware of limits on its natural resources, a decline in global security, and its failure, so far, to solve the great worries of non-stop inflation."[6] But it is also the same "land of dreams" it has always been, where omnipotent fantasies of the good life compete with warnings of hard times ahead.

Inflation's Effects on Nation's Well-Being

Few economists dispute the conventional wisdom that Americans will make more money in the 1980s — and pay more for the things they buy. But there does seem to be two schools of thought on how the overall economy will fare in the next decade. Looking beyond rising inflation and uncertain credit prospects for the immediate future, some experts are forecasting a commercial boom. "An expanding population, with rising income levels, will provide merchants with a huge market in the Eighties," predicted the Morgan Guaranty Trust Co. of New York. "Even for those long accustomed to big numbers, [the decade] should be impressive. Americans will have to get used to analysts routinely bandying about ever-bigger measures of sales and production: 17 million new cars and trucks in one year, 2-1/2 million new houses a year and so on."[7]

However, the people who presumably will be purchasing those

---

[3] Robert G. Kaiser and Jon Lowell, writing in *The Washington Post*, July 29, 1979.
[4] *Time* magazine, May 28, 1978, p. 39. Writer Tom Wolfe introduced the much-used term "me decade" in a *New York* magazine article in 1976.
[5] Richard Reeves, writing in *Esquire* magazine, November 1979.
[6] *U.S. News & World Report*, Oct. 15, 1979, p. 45.
[7] *The Morgan Guaranty Survey*, February 1979, p. 10.

items appear more circumspect about what the economy promises. In a recent *New York Times*/CBS News Poll, 40 percent of those interviewed cited continuing severe inflation as the most pressing problem the nation will face in the 1980s. Less than half as many believed the energy crisis would be more important. Decisive action by government officials might cap the spiraling prices, they said. But many complained about the country's lack of determined economic leadership.[8] *Fortune* magazine, in looking at "the decade ahead," finds the American middle class so anxious about inflation "that the government will be compelled to adopt effective inflation-slowing policies. And there is evidence that the 'fed-up' point [in public opinion] may not be so very far off."[9]

"I want to talk to you ... about a fundamental threat to American democracy. ... It is a crisis of confidence. ... The erosion of our confidence in the future is threatening to destroy the social and political fabric of America."

President Carter
July 15, 1979

Double-digit inflation, which has been an economic constant in the closing year of the 1970s, is responsible for sharp rises in the price of housing, transportation, food and clothing. In addition, American budgets have been squeezed by rising Social Security payments[10] and higher federal income taxes that come with increased earnings. The Conference Board, an independent economic research organization, reported in May that the average family now must earn almost double its 1970 pre-tax income to maintain the same standard of living it had then. Some forecasters have said that this year's rate of inflation, currently running at 13 percent, will probably drop to 5 percent by 1990. But economists are unsure how much gain there will be in real purchasing power — after subtracting for taxes and inflation.

Keeping pace with rising costs already has forced a number of significant changes in the lives of many Americans, changes that observers expect to continue into the next decade. The most pronounced alteration seems to have occurred within the family.

---

[8] *New York Times*/CBS News Poll, Oct. 19, 1979.
[9] William Bowen, "The Decade Ahead: Not So Bad If We Do Things Right," *Fortune*, Oct. 8, 1979, p. 88.
[10] See "Social Security Reassessment," *E.R.R.*, 1979 Vol. I, pp. 461-480.

Among the 48 million husband-wife households, about half of the wives work.

"Most [women] don't have the option of working inside the home or outside the home anymore," said Alexis M. Herman, director of the Women's Bureau of the Labor Department. "Economic needs require that they go out and get a job." The Urban Institute, a Washington-based research firm, predicts that by 1990, more than 55 percent (52 million) of all women aged 16 and older will be in the work force. This will include two-thirds of all married women under 55 and more than half the mothers with children under age six. The economic effects of inflation are for the most part easily apparent. But the long-term implications of so many women working outside the home, said sociologist Eli Ginzberg, "are absolutely unchartable."[11]

Country's Emerging Conservative Temper

"Proposition 13" — the words began ringing like a death knell in the ears of many public officials in the late 1970s, tolling an end to unchecked spending and the approach of a new era of fiscal restraint. Approval of the ballot proposal by California voters in June 1978 cut that state's property tax revenue in half and started a nationwide movement to reduce the taxing power of state and local governments. On Nov. 6, 1979, California voters approved a new measure — Proposition 4 — that places ceilings on state spending. Backers predict that it, too, will be imitated in other states.

While some people see anti-spending initiatives as a manifestation of inflation-bred "stinginess," others have identified them as part of a counter-attack on big government by the taxpaying public — further evidence, they say, of a growing conservative mood in the country at large. In his book *The Neo-Conservatives* (1979), author Peter Steinfels portrays the nation gradually turning to the right and sees this as a "reaction to sixties turbulence, an outlook fierce in its attachment to political and cultural moderation . . . pessimistic about the possibilities for long- or even short-range change in America, and imbued with a foreboding sense of our civilization's decline." According to Steinfels, the new conservatism is connected, both emotionally and intellectually, to the same sense of "things in disorder" now gaining so much currency.[12]

A Gallup Poll conducted early in November indicated that almost half of the people questioned (47 percent) considered themselves conservatives while only 32 percent saw themselves as liberals. Needless to say, political conservatism takes many

[11] Quoted by Caroline Bird in *Two-Paycheck Family* (1979), pp. xii-xiii. See also "Women in the Work Force," *E.R.R.,* 1977 Vol. I, pp. 121-142.

[12] For an elaboration of this view, see Christopher Lasch's *The Culture of Narcissism: American Life in an Age of Diminishing Expectations* (1978).

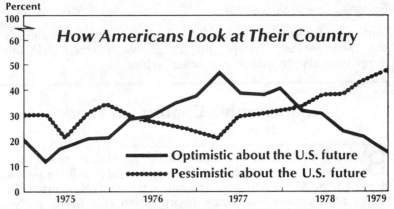

Percent

How Americans Look at Their Country

——— **Optimistic about the U.S. future**
•••••••• **Pessimistic about the U.S. future**

1975 1976 1977 1978 1979

SOURCE: Surveys by Cambridge Reports, published in *Public Opinion* magazine, October-November 1979.

forms, but there is general agreement on certain core elements of the conservative position. Primarily, it stands for preservation of an existing system of government or traditional standards of moral and cultural judgment. Change, most conservatives believe, should evolve "naturally" as a result of the unfolding of new social conditions. "It is a common theme of conservatism," wrote author Irving Howe, "to urge caution, even inaction, on the ground that action leads to unforeseen and usually undesirable consequences."[13] Whereas liberals are wont to see themselves as reformers, conservatives tend to consider themselves guardians of an established order.

Conservative feelings often do not translate into votes. Arthur M. Schlesinger Jr., the historian identified with political liberalism, contends that the current swing to the right lies mostly in the realm of "notional assent."[14] However, as anger over tax inequities, legalized abortions, reverse discrimination and homosexual and women's rights continues to become more vocal, "notional assent" could take on a more active form.

As prosperity recedes, a large class of working Americans who once embraced civil rights and social welfare legislation now seems less partial to liberal-spirited largess. In the 1970s, the economic interests of this class have gained considerable influence on the direction of government, whose role as a provider seems to have changed in recent years to that of a conservator.

In the next decade, many observers feel, continuing discontent over waste and inefficiency in many institutions will impel public officials to seek even more ways to constrain government rather than expand its benefits. If, as some social critics contend, inflation and economic uncertainty have made Americans more devoted to the accumulation of material goods,

[13] Irving Howe, "The Right Menace," *The New Republic*, Sept. 9, 1978, p. 4.
[14] In *The Wall Street Journal*, Feb. 21, 1978.

sentiment for sharing the wealth is likely to further diminish in the 1980s, as more people put their own interests first and everything else in descending order behind it.

Demographic Changes at Work

B Y THE CLOSE of the 1980s, assuming that no major wars or epidemics occur, there will be close to 243 million people living in the United States, according to the U.S. Census Bureau's most-favoed line range of projection *(see table, p. 10)*. That means an increase of about 9.5 percent over the present 222 million, which would be the smallest rate of growth since 1940.

If present trends hold, Americans will continue moving around the country, claiming a new address every five years on average. There will also be more unmarried couples moving in together, if the social habits of the Seventies don't suffer an abrupt change. The Census Bureau reports that the number of couples living together without the bonds of matrimony has doubled in the past 10 years. The divorce rate is likely to continue to go up and the birth rate to continue to go down. There will, no doubt, be a further drop in the number of young children and a further increase in the number of older people.

The rate at which Americans come into the world and the ages at which they leave it are working a radical transformation in the makeup of the population. In fact, the changing age structure of the country will make the status of the elderly a central issue for years to come. The number of persons over 65, the age at which most people become eligible for retirement, has been increasing steadily throughout this century. In 1900, there were 3.1 million persons 65 or older, constituting 4 percent of the population. By 1975, their ranks had swollen to 22.4 million, constituting one-tenth of the nation.

But this gradual increase seems small compared with the rapid rise expected over the next several decades. Like a tidal wave approaching shore, the growing numbers of older people may be headed for a devastating collision with society's systems of caring for them.

That demographic bulge is a product of the postwar "baby boom." During the years following World War II, the United States experienced an unprecedented upsurge in fertility, peaking at a record 4.3 million births in 1957. Actually, the years before the baby-boomers reach retirement will be relatively easy ones for income security. The year 1980 will be the

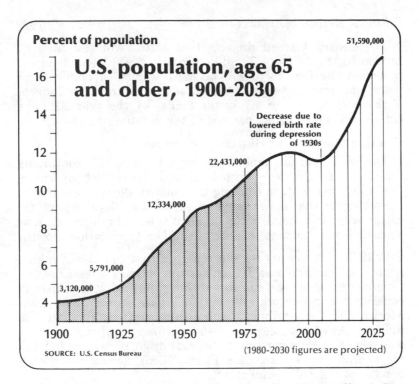

Percent of population

U.S. population, age 65 and older, 1900-2030

51,590,000

Decrease due to lowered birth rate during depression of 1930s

22,431,000

12,334,000

5,791,000

3,120,000

1900   1925   1950   1975   2000   2025

SOURCE: U.S. Census Bureau   (1980-2030 figures are projected)

peak year for persons in the 18-24 age bracket (29.5 million). But by 1995, because of declining fertility in the last decade or so, this age group is expected to shrink to 23.2 million. Consequently the competition for jobs and college entry should lessen.[15]

The 1990s and the early years of the next millenium will also show a similar decline in the proportion of aged Americans. That will be the time those born during the relatively infertile depression years of the 1930s turn 65. After about 2010, however, the number of elderly will rise swiftly as the baby-boomers begin to turn 65. Demographers now think the total will hit about 52 million in 2030, and then hold steady or decline after that.

The growing percentage of aged persons in this country is often referred to as "the graying of America." Contrary to a common belief, America is becoming gray not so much because people are living longer but because younger people are having so few children. After the end of the postwar baby boom, and with the introduction of oral contraceptives, the birth rate declined rapidly. Demographers call these the "baby bust" years. By 1976 the average number of births for each woman had fallen to 1.7 — well below the 2.1 average needed over the long run to maintain a stable population.

---

[15] See *Domestic Consequences of United States Population Change,* Select Committee on Population, U.S. House of Representatives, December 1978.

The Census Bureau projects that births will rise from 33 million in the 1970s to 39 million in the 1980s. This change is based on the fact there will be more women of childbearing years, not from any expected increase in the birth rate. Indeed, if the current rate of 1.7 births holds, by the year 2030 the elderly will make up 22 percent of the population.

Growing Numbers of Hispanic-Americans

The wild card in population projections is the continuing influx of immigrants — both legal and illegal. Nobody knows how many persons are entering the country illegally each year. According to the higher range of estimates, illegal aliens, together with an annual influx of 400,000 legal immigrants, now account for 50 percent or more of the U.S. population growth.

In 1970, the Census Bureau reported that Spanish-speaking Americans had replaced Italians as the nation's largest linguistic minority. However, the size of this group today is subject to considerable guesswork; it contains illegal immigrants from Mexico and the Caribbean whose numbers may run into the millions. As of last year, the Census Bureau's official estimate was that 12 million persons of Hispanic origin or descent lived in the United States (excluding Puerto Rico), accounting for 5.6 percent of the U.S. population.

Census Bureau Projections

The Census Bureau makes three population forecasts, each based on a different assumption as to birth rates. The following table shows the three projections:

(population in millions)

	Series I	Series II	Series III
1980	224.1	222.2	220.7
1990	254.1	243.5	236.3

Series I — the highest projection — assumes that the average number of births per woman will be 2.7. Series II assumes 2.1 average births per woman — close to the "replacement level" associated with zero population growth. Series III assumes an average of 1.7 births per woman.

The birth rate has dropped below even the zero population growth rate. However, demographers do not expect a long-term continuation of the sharp decline that has taken place in the birth rate. Rather, they think the most reasonable assumption for the long run is a replacement-level birth rate — the Series II projection.

Seven million of this group were Mexican-Americans, concentrated mainly in the southwestern rim of states stretching from Texas to California. The growth among the Hispanic population is such that some demographers believe it may constitute the nation's largest minority in the 1980s, pushing American blacks into second place. Blacks now total about 26 million, making up 11.8 percent of the U.S. population. By the end of the 1980s, they are expected to number 30 million or 12.2 percent.[16]

Since it doesn't know how many are coming into the country, the Census Bureau chooses not to include illegal aliens in its population projections. In the past, most immigrants have been young. And if this holds true for the illegal immigrants, it means that they will be a significant factor in the work force through the 1980s and beyond.

'Sun Belt' Lure and Big City Renaissance

It has been called "the second War between the States." What it really amounts to, though, is desertion — populations leaving the older, colder urban centers of the Northeast and Midwest for the newer cities of the "Sun Belt." "As long as the migration of industry and population was gradual from what was a relatively rich Northeast to what was a relatively impoverished South and Southwest, it helped to unify the country," *Business Week* magazine concluded in 1976. "But within the past five years, the process has burst beyond the bounds that can be accommodated by existing political institutions."[17]

An increase in the movement of jobs and people southward in the 1980s does not necessarily mean that the northern states will suffer a drop in income or standard of living. On the contrary, "the [reverse] may be reasonably argued," wrote Richard B. McKenzie, professor of economics at Clemson University. The southern migration has actually benefited the North, he contended. "By moving South, where production costs are lower, industries are able to provide goods and services to northern markets at lower prices than they would . . . if they had stayed in the North."[18]

Nevertheless, as southern and southwestern cities like Atlanta, Orlando, Houston, Phoenix and San Diego continue to increase their populations, while most northern cities are losing theirs, demographic shifts will inevitably result in political changes. When the 1980 census figures are used to reapportion Congress, a majority of the members of the House of Represen-

[16] See *Population Profile of the United States: 1978,* Bureau of the Census, April 1979.

[17] "The Second War between the States," *Business Week,* May 17, 1976, p. 92.

[18] Richard B. McKenzie, "Restrictions on Business Mobility: A Study in Political Rhetoric and Economic Reality," *American Enterprise Institute Studies in Economic Policy* (1979), p. 26.

tatives for the first time in the nation's history are likely to be southerners and westerners.

A bright spot in the population picture for East Coast and midwestern urban centers is the "back to the city" movement. Little by little, the middle class is returning to the long-neglected cities, restoring dilapidated property and revitalizing stagnant economies. While the displacement of minority residents is a problem yet to be solved, many northern officials are looking to private reinvestment in urban neighborhoods as one form of renewal that may save America's cities in the 1980s.

Neighborhoods As a Base of Local Power

A generation ago, the day-to-day problems in many American cities were solved by calling a ward captain; leaves were picked up, trash collected, street lights repaired. All that was asked in return was a vote. But those days, most observers agree, are gone. Traditional local institutions have broken down, they say, and neighborhood organizations are taking over. "Neighborhoods can perform all sorts of functions that distant government cannot," said Milton Kotler, director of the Washington-based National Association of Neighborhoods. "In the future, they will be shouldering a greater responsibility for public assistance and public economy than we can ever imagine."

The burgeoning "neighborhood power" movement, an outgrowth in one sense of the local activism of the late 1960s, has many variations. But a common thread is the desire of people to make more of the decisions that directly affect their communities and thus their lives. In Washington, D.C., Hartford, Conn., Newark, N.J., and other large and small cities across the country, neighborhood organizations are assuming tasks once handled by local governments — housing rehabilitation, crime control, even schooling — and in many cases doing a better job. "What we are seeing is the evolution of the city ward system into a more responsive, more efficient mechanism for helping people," Kotler said.

The old machine performed needed services. But it always seemed to work best for those who paid their political dues. Neighborhood organizations are, by contrast, avowedly non-ideological. Their interest is promoting community cooperation through a kind of "higher" neighborliness. "We are trying to assist people who live near each other learn to live close to each other," said Terry Snapp, a local activist from Independence, Mo. What is taking place, some social theorists believe, is a literal working out on the community level of the "smaller is better" philosophy.

In an age when political power is being subdivided into smaller and smaller parcels, neighborhood organizations in the 1980s could have an important influence on local elections. Big city mayors who have already risen to office with their support include Seattle's Charles Royer, Atlanta's Maynard Jackson and Chicago's Jane Byrne. So strong are Byrne's ties to community groups in Chicago that one of her first official acts was to fulfill a campaign pledge by proposing the creation of a municipal Department of Neighborhoods. If approved by the city council, it would be the first such department in the nation.

In March 1979, a presidentially-appointed National Commission on Neighborhoods, after a two-year study of urban communities, recommended the restructuring of existing government programs to meet the future needs of neighborhoods and their people. The commission said it "believes that government should support neighborhood initiatives and that it should sustain the level of programs that do or could meet neighborhood needs."[19] Instead of calling for massive new federal assistance, the commission urged increased involvement of neighborhood residents and organizations in planning and carrying out programs that serve them. Neighborhoods want political independence and economic self-sufficiency, the report concluded; they should no longer be treated as "colonies" continually dependent for their well-being on government "handouts."

Reshaping Suburbia's Mentality, Landscape

If city neighborhoods of the 1980s are likely to be different from their predecessors of a generation ago, the suburbs also can be expected to undergo significant changes. The energy shortage, increased population density and the added fiscal burdens brought on by more residents all have begun to reshape the landscape of suburbia. The "isolationist" mentality that used to prevail, while it has not entirely disappeared, has been tempered as suburbanites are beginning to admit social and economic realities that in years past might have easily gone ignored.

From 1970 to 1978, the suburban population increased by 12.3 percent, according to Census Bureau findings. Growth is sure to continue in the 1980s. But the suburbs face a problem of absorbing newcomers. There is only so much space available for new residents. And many suburban areas — some of which have taken steps to slow development — have already reached their limits.

The theory that urban and suburban problems are vastly dissimilar has lost much of its credibility among many experts who are now urging local, state and federal officials to develop

---

[19] See *People Building Neighborhoods*, National Commission on Neighborhoods, 1979.

long-range regional development programs to help cities and their surrounding areas cope with the problems of growth. Michigan recently installed what some observers regard as a model city-suburban revenue-sharing program; the state subsidizes services that Detroit and its suburbs use. In California, lawmakers are attempting to revive a bill defeated two years ago to conserve open spaces in the path of suburban expansion. In Massachusetts, officials have developed a comprehensive strategy to help cities and small towns deal with shifting populations. The state has also enacted legislation to curtail highway construction, which in the past paved the way for new housing construction and far-flung industrial development.

Neal R. Peirce, a syndicated columnist who writes on the problems of cities, sees such planning essential in the coming decades. "Unless the last several years' pattern of growth at the suburban fringe is curbed," established urban centers might lose more than "a third of their populations by the end of the century."[20]

To keep usable farmland from being lost to development, a number of counties — notably Suffolk in New York, Howard in Maryland and King in Washington — have begun to purchase acreage lying in the path of expanding suburban areas. Similar preventive measures have been put into operation in Honolulu, Minneapolis-St. Paul and Portland, Ore. But the majority of local governments have fallen behind these cities in protecting land from future unchecked development.

While containing growth is certain to become an even more urgent task in the 1980s, it conflicts with the most allowed of all American aspirations — owning one's own home on one's own plot of ground. It is that desire that gave rise to metropolitan sprawl. And before haphazard expansion can be brought under control, that dream may have to be deferred for the foreseeable future.

Political Contours of a Decade

CONSIDERING the nature of the presidency, novelist-critic Wilfrid Sheed has observed, "it's hard to imagine it was ever designed for a human."[21] There is, of course, an irony in this, since campaigns for the White House now are almost totally dominated by "personalities," by what candidates say or imply about their "human" qualities and those of their opponents.

[20] Neal R. Peirce, writing in the Baltimore *Sun,* July 11, 1979.
[21] Wilfrid Sheed, *The Good Word and Other Words* (1979), p. 79.

Presidential Commission on the 1980s

President Carter in October 1979 created the Commission for a National Agenda for the 1980s. Consisting of 26 members* and headed by the outgoing president of Columbia University, Dr. William J. McGill, the commission will examine energy, inflation, productivity, demographics and other pertinent national matters and report its recommendations sometime next year. Hedley W. Donovan, former editor-in-chief of Time Inc. and now a senior White House adviser, will serve as special liaison to the group. The project is important in "developing a sense of long-range vision and purpose" for the country, Donovan said. International affairs will be "looked at only to the extent that they affect domestic areas," he added.

Previous administrations also set future objectives for the government. At the end of his second term, President Eisenhower established the Commission on National Goals that recommended, among other things, overhauling the tax system and ending racial discrimination in higher education. President Johnson shortly after taking office set up 16 task forces in 1964 to suggest new directions in federal policy. Many of their recommendations subsequently became part of Johnson's Great Society program of the mid-1960s.

The idea of conducting a formal study of the 1980s evolved out of President Carter's meetings with dozens of business, labor and political leaders at Camp David last July. Donovan emphasized, however, that "it might be presumptuous to suppose that 21 people can sit down and figure out precisely where the country ought to be in 10 years." Once the commission begins its work, he said, "it will hold meetings at various places around the nation and invite participation and suggestions from the public."

*In addition to McGill: Daniel Bell, professor of Sociology at Harvard University; J. Fred Bucy Jr., president, Texas Instruments; Pastora San Juan Cafferty, professor of the School of Social Service, University of Chicago; Elizabeth Carpenter, consultant, LBJ Library, Austin, Texas; Marian Edelman, director, Children's Defense Fund; John Gardner, founding chairman, Common Cause; Philip Handler, president, National Academy of Sciences; Dorothy Height, president, National Council of Negro Women; Ruth Hinerfeld, president, League of Women Voters; Matina Horner, president, Radcliffe College; Carl Holman, president, National Urban Coalition; Rhoda Karpatkin, president of Consumers Union; Lane Kirkland, AFL-CIO president; Juanita Kreps, former Secretary of Commerce; Esther Landa, President's Advisory Committee for Women; Michael McCloskey, Sierra Club executive director; Bill Moyers, television commentator; Frank Pace, International Executive Service Corps; Donald Platten, chairman, Chemical Bank; Elspeth Rostow, dean, LBJ School of Public Affairs, University of Texas; Howard Samuels, business consultant, Howard Samuels Enterprises; Henry Schacht, president, Cummins Engine Co.; William Scranton, former governor of Pennsylvania; Glenn Watts, president, Communications Workers of America; Marina Whitman, vice president, General Motors.

"The 1980s," wrote *Washington Post* columnist Haynes Johnson, "could prove to be the most critical decade of this century in terms of the issues facing America. . . . Yet it seems certain the candidates [in the 1980 presidential campaign] won't be debating issues or ideology."[22] What they will probably be talk-

---

[22] Haynes Johnson, writing in *The Washington Post*, Nov. 4, 1979.

ing about more than anything else, Johnson ventured, is one another.

For most of America's history, the party was the ultimate vehicle for political expression. While parties still provide the nominal framework within which candidates do battle, it became increasingly clear in the 1970s that parties had lost a good deal of their former control over politicians and voters. The disappearance of strong central party organizations may, as some have said, bestow welcomed benefits, such as affording citizens greater access to the political process. But with the old partisan coalitions in disarray, elections — particularly presidential elections — have become a validation of the man, not the party. New campaign rules and a new political climate have placed personal questions above platform issues.

"The predisposition [to have confidence in] our leaders, despite some of the things we know about them," wrote journalist Elizabeth Drew, "bespeaks an understanding that every free society has to proceed on trust."[23] In the mid-1970s, though, the Watergate scandal destroyed a large part of that trust and in the process altered the public's outlook on the presidency. During the 1976 presidential campaign, the circumstances surrounding President Nixon's resignation required that Gerald R. Ford and Jimmy Carter prove themselves not only competent but personally fit to be president.

It is generally agreed that Carter won the election on the strength of his promise to return honesty and integrity to government. Even so, analysts have speculated whether post-Watergate distrust of the presidency might lead the public and the press to expect too much of any man holding the office. With the 1980 campaign already under way, that theory is sure to be tested. And the president's own party could be the proving ground, as Carter and Sen. Edward M. Kennedy, D-Mass., his principal challenger, contend for the nomination.

SALT: Symbol of Shared Global Power

When the 1980 presidential election is consigned to history, the winner will have to deal with a world of multiple problems. The rise of terrorism, the steady depletion of the Earth's resources, the economic strains on governments everywhere — these are the global realities. Given the plight of the American economy and this country's declining prestige abroad, determining a proper overseas role for the United States in the 1980s promises to be no easy matter.

Many of the hopes and anxieties over America's future position in the world are summarized in the terms as well as the

---

[23] Elizabeth Drew, *Washington Journal: The Events of 1973-1974* (1975), p. 360.

Think-Tank Futurology

"Virtually the only subject that a futurologist will not talk about readily is his batting average. Nobody pays a think tank to tote up its past performance, and trepidation has prevented most of the groups from doing so on their own.

"Most of them have done a competent job of discussing the consequences of basic modern trends. . . . But ask them to recall a specific long-range forecast that correctly foresaw a change in trend, and the futurologists get evasive. They . . . have missed, pretty much to a man, the major upheavals that have largely shaped the past decade.

"Economist Lester Thurow sums up the failure of forecasting: 'These people would be useful only if they could tell us about change. But did any of them predict the war in Vietnam, the sudden drop in the growth rate of population, the advent of structural inflation, or the intensity of the entrance of women in the work force?' Nor did the most important event of the 1970s, the quadrupling of oil prices in 1973, come in for more than feeble adumbration."

—James Taub, writing in
Saturday Review, December 1979

implications of the Strategic Arms Limitation Treaty (SALT II) between the world's two nuclear superpowers, the United States and Russia. In its most important sense, the treaty before the Senate for approval is "almost entirely symbolic," said diplomatic historian Ronald Steel.[24] Under "the umbrella of a nuclear standoff," he added, SALT is a metaphor for détente, the strength of U.S. economic alliances and its status in the Third World. On paper, the agreements impose maximum levels on U.S. and Soviet strategic power.[25] But the treaty's implications go far beyond that. It implicitly declares the fate of the world to be in the hands of two nations, either one of which could destroy the other at a moment's notice.

The way opponents perceive each other's strong points and weaknesses lies at the heart of the diplomatic bargaining process. "Credibility," wrote author Strobe Talbott, "is the essence of both arms buildups and control measures. . . . [One side's weapons] are meant to convince the other side that it cannot use its arms without incurring catastrophic retaliation."[26] The credibility of SALT, however, seems inexorably linked to a whole series of events, not directly related to talks themselves, that reflect U.S. and Russian strength relative to one another and, increasingly, to the rest of the world.

---

[24] Ronald Steel, writing in *The Washington Post*, Oct. 21, 1979.
[25] See "Strategic Arms Debate," *E.R.R.*, 1979 Vol. I, pp. 401-420.
[26] Strobe Talbott, *Endgame: The Inside Story of SALT II* (1979), p. 29.

SALT comes at "a time of trial" for American interests around the world. Soviet intervention in Africa, the presence of Russian troops in Cuba, the taking of American hostages in Iran, the dollar drain to pay for imported oil, all conspire to give the appearance of confirming a decline in U.S. power and influence.

"The 1980s have already begun," declares Irving Kristol, the conservative philosopher, writing on the editorial page of the Nov. 26 *Wall Street Journal*. "They began with the takeover of the American embassy in Tehran earlier this month [Nov. 4] and with the subsequent confrontation of the United States with a virulently anti-Western Iranian regime. This episode is . . . the shocking prologue to an equally tense drama that stands poised to unfold in the decade ahead. It promises to be an absolutely ghastly period."

Rise and Decline of the American Century

Time magazine founder Henry Luce called this "the American Century." Now, according to some thinkers, it may be coming to an early end. America has "had a tremendous and pervasive cultural influence," said British historian Paul Johnson. "American attitudes — the notion of plenty, the notion of mass production being a common legacy; that if you worked hard enough you could, in the end, get what you wanted — were the keynote of the world."[27] The 1970s, however, saw both a reduction in America's role as a foreign power and a gearing down of the U.S. economic dynamo. Inflation plagued the dollar at home and abroad and American productivity was too sluggish to overcome inflation's effects. Productivity — output per worker — rose during the 1970s at only one-third the rate that it did during the 1960s.

In the decade that will see George Orwell's dreaded 1984 come and go, the pessimists may outnumber the optimists. Herman Kahn of the Hudson Institute, normally the most optimistic of "think tank" seers, has recently voiced some doubts about the 1980s, a decade which he had pictured glowingly in his bicentennial year book *The Next Two Hundred Years*. Last summer he told *U.S. News & World Report:* "We will be a bit more disaster-prone . . . less able to absorb shocks without discomfort. . . . Arteriosclerosis has already set in. Our reaction time is slowing when a crisis arises, and our policy-makers tend to flounder."[28]

The public's reaction to what Kahn sees as "gloom at the top," has been, by many accounts, a suspicion that things are slipping out of control. Yet a Gallup Poll taken last March

---

[27] "Is the American Century Ending: Conversations with Paul Johnson and Daniel Boorstin," *Public Opinion*, March-May 1979.

[28] Quoted in *U.S. News & World Report*, Aug. 20, 1979, pp. 52-53.

The Coming Orwellian Decade

Since its publication 30 years ago, George Orwell's novel *1984* has been a code word for a nightmarish future in which lies become the official truth. Orwell's elaborate satire on modern politics is a vision of the world dehumanized by thought control and laid waste by warring dictators.

The grim events he portrays take place in the year 1984. It is said that Orwell chose the year for his book title quite whimsically. He was writing the book during 1948, and so decided to transpose the year's last two numerals.

1984

Literary critics say the book reflected Orwell's distrust of all political parties — as gained from a lifetime of experience. The son of a colonial official in India, Eric Blair (Orwell's real name) acquired an abiding distaste for the class system during his English schooling and lived much of his life among the poor, about whom he wrote. A leftist who fought with the Republicans in the Spanish Civil War, he quickly became disillusioned and anti-communist. Orwell died in 1950 at age 47.

"The novel [*1984*]," said a recent appraisal,* "kept the whole notion of the 80s-to-come alive for a generation of readers, forewarning them to reject Big Brother lest the world of that decade turn out to be positively, well, Orwellian."

*By Glenn Collins in *Psychology Today,* January 1979, p. 34.

points up the resilient nature of the American claim to happiness even in the midst of predictions of oncoming woe. While 69 percent of those interviewed expressed dissatisfaction with the prospects of the nation as a whole, 77 percent said they were hopeful about their own personal futures. Most people, the poll seems to suggest, continue to expect "more" despite their feelings that the 1980s will be a time of "less."

The future has always been a favorite refuge for Americans. It beckons, novelist F. Scott Fitzgerald wrote in *The Great Gatsby* (1925), like some elusive dream "that year by year recedes before us." But the luxury of keeping up the pursuit may no longer be an available alternative to living with the demands of "lower expectations." Growth, expansion, ease and comfort have been national commandments for generations. Whether they remain part of the popular cargo of beliefs a decade from now could depend on how well, after years of looking in the other direction, Americans are able to face reality in the 1980s.

Selected Bibliography

Books

Bird, Caroline, *The Two-Paycheck Family,* Rawson, Wade Publishers, 1979.

Brown, Lester R., *The Twenty-Ninth Day,* Norton, 1978.

Crowe, Kenneth, *America for Sale,* Doubleday & Co., 1978.

Erdman, Paul, *The Crash of '79,* Simon & Schuster, 1976.

Hendra, Tony, Christopher Cerf and Peter Elbling (eds.), *The 80s: A Look Back at the Tumultuous Decade, 1980-1989,* Workman Press, 1979.

Kaiser, Robert G. and Jon Lowell, *Great American Dreams,* Harper & Row, 1979.

Kemp, Jack, *The American Renaissance: A Strategy for the 80s,* Harper & Row, 1979.

Lasch, Christopher, *The Culture of Narcissism: American Life in an Age of Diminishing Expectations,* Norton, 1978.

Muller, Herbert J., *Uses of the Future,* Indiana University Press, 1974.

Toffler, Alvin, *Future Shock,* Random House, 1970.

World Future Society, *The Next 25 Years: Crisis and Opportunity,* 1975.

Articles

"Challenges of the 80s," *U.S. News & World Report,* Oct. 15, 1979.

"Decade of Promise — or Problems?" *The Morgan Guarantee Survey,* February 1979.

"Ennui the People," *The New Republic,* Aug. 4-11, 1979.

"Is the American Century Ending: Conversations with Paul Johnson and Daniel Boorstin," *Public Opinion,* March-May 1979.

Murphy, Thomas A., "Is America Ready for the 80s?" (speech delivered at the National Coal Association Convention, Colorado Springs, Colo., June 22, 1979), *Vital Speeches of the Day,* Aug. 1, 1979.

Satow, Roberta, "Pop Narcissism," *Psychology Today,* October 1979.

"Tomorrow's Growth Industries," *Dun's Review,* February 1979.

Reports and Studies

Cohen, Rick, "Localism: Research Themes on Urban Smallness," Institute on Man and Science and the Charles F. Kettering Foundation, 1979.

Editorial Research Reports: "America's Next Century," 1976 Vol. I, p. 1; "Challenges for the 1970s," 1969 Vol. II, p. 855.

Joint Economic Committee of Congress, "U.S. Long-Term Economic Growth Prospects: Entering a New Era," Jan. 25, 1978.

Rooney, Robert F. and M. Bruce Johnson, "The Economics of America's Third Century," International Institute for Economic Research, 1979.

Nov. 16
1 9 7 9

CLOSING THE ENVIRONMENTAL DECADE

by

William Sweet

Vol. II
No. 18

CLOSING THE ENVIRONMENTAL DECADE

NEW YEAR'S DAY 1980 will mark the tenth anniversary of the National Environmental Policy Act (NEPA), which had as its principal objective the encouragement of a "productive and enjoyable harmony between man and his environment." President Nixon made the NEPA signing ceremony on Jan. 1, 1970, his first official act of the new decade, saying that "the 1970s absolutely must be the years when America pays its debt to the past by reclaiming the purity of its air, its waters, and our living environment."[1] Many Americans agreed that the environment deserved far greater attention, and on April 22, 1970, less than four months after Nixon inaugurated the environmental decade, thousands of people gathered in cities and communities around the country to celebrate Earth Day.

Now that the Seventies are drawing to a close, many of the people who first met on Earth Day to demonstrate in favor of a better environment are planning to commemorate the occasion and celebrate the achievements of the past decade. But the festivities may be somewhat muted. For there is widespread fear that environmental concerns will fare poorly in the Eighties, as efforts to augment domestic energy supplies and reduce the costs associated with pollution abatement loom ever larger in the nation's affairs. President Carter, who received some of his strongest support from conservationists during his first two years in office, now is in trouble with environmentalists largely because of his attempts to expedite energy projects of urgent national interest.

To be sure, Americans are most unlikely to revert in the next decade to the habits of an era in which the quality of their air, water and land received little or no attention. In contrast to the situation 10 years ago, when environmentalists were widely regarded as kooky hippies who wanted to give up all the gifts of modern industrial civilization for the sake of returning to a mythical world of plants and animals, environmentalism today is firmly entrenched in the nation's consciousness. The jargon of environmentalism — "ecological balance," "recycling," "renewable resources" — has become a part of every educated person's working vocabulary. The small groups of activists who organized Earth Day in 1970 have developed into large, highly professional

---

[1] See "Environmental Policy," *E.R.R.*, 1974 Vol. II, pp. 945-964.

organizations. But such organizations probably will be working under increasingly adverse conditions in the Eighties, and most environmentalists doubt that the major legislative achievements of the 1970s will be duplicated in the next decade.

Major Legislation of the Past Ten Years

In the post-World War II period as a whole, only the civil rights legislation of the mid-1960s and the national security legislation of the late 1940s rival in importance the body of environmental legislation enacted during the Seventies. In addition to improving federal policy in certain traditional areas of environmental concern, such as land management and protection of endangered species *(see box)*, Congress authorized the establishment of new environmental procedures and agencies, passed laws to clean up the nation's air and water, and took steps to eliminate toxic chemicals from the environment. This corpus of legislation by itself would justify calling the Seventies the environmental decade.

The law which ushered in the decade, the National Environmental Policy Act, has been called an environmental "bill of rights" or "Magna Carta." Its most important provision required federal agencies to assess the effects of any "major federal action affecting the environment." In establishing the environmental impact statement, NEPA put a powerful tool into the hands of environmentalists. Individuals and groups now could challenge federal projects in the courts on the basis that the environmental impact had been inadequately assessed, and as it turned out the courts tended throughout the Seventies to enforce the law's requirements rigorously.

NEPA also established the Council on Environmental Quality to advise the president and to act as a kind of environmental ombudsman. Less than a year after the Council was set up, President Nixon recommended the establishment of the Environmental Protection Agency. EPA, which started operations on Dec. 2, 1970, took over responsibility for implementing environmental policies and for setting environmental standards for numerous federal agencies, including the National Air Pollution Control Administration, the Food and Drug Administration, and the Atomic Energy Commission. New legislation enacted in the following years greatly augmented EPA's responsibilities.

The Clean Air Act of 1970 set a schedule for reduction of automobile pollutants,[2] established federally enforced primary air-quality standards and state-enforced secondary standards, required states to prepare implementation plans for meeting secondary standards, and gave EPA the authority to rule on the

---

[2] See "Auto Emission Controls," *E.R.R.*, 1973 Vol. I, pp. 289-312.

Other Environmental Laws of the 1970s

Important environmental legislation enacted in the Seventies included, in addition to NEPA and pollution-control bills, the following laws:

Occupational Safety and Health Act of 1970. Authorized the secretary of labor, acting through the Occupational Safety and Health Administration, to set standards which employers must obey, including standards for toxics such as benzene, asbestos dust, vinyl chloride, cotton dust, and coke oven emissions.

Alaska Native Claims Settlement Act of 1971. Allowed the government to set aside 80 million acres of land in Alaska as national parks, forests and wildlife refuges.

Federal Environmental Pesticide Control Act of 1972. Required registration of all pesticides with the Environmental Protection Agency, which would be responsible for controlling their manufacture, distribution, and use.

Endangered Species Act of 1973. Prohibited federal projects that would destroy or modify a habitat crucial to the survival of an endangered species.

Safe Drinking Water Act of 1974. Directed the Environmental Protection Agency to set maximum levels for certain chemical and bacteriological pollutants.

Federal Land Policy and Management Act of 1976. Updated and consolidated about 3,000 public laws pertaining to management of federal lands by the Bureau of Land Management.

Federal Mine Safety and Health Act of 1977. Transferred regulatory authority over all types of mines from the Department of Interior to the Department of Labor, applied a single statute to both coal and non-coal mines, expedited procedures for setting standards, imposing penalties and collecting fines, and included a toxics provision to assure "the highest degree of health and safety protection."

Surface Mining Control and Reclamation Act of 1977. Set performance standards to be met by all major coal strip-mining operations and protected certain lands as unsuitable for surface mining.

adequacy of state plans. Congress revised standards and extended deadlines several times after 1970, notably in the Energy Supply and Environmental Coordination Act of 1974 and the Clean Air Amendments of 1977, but the basic policy of reducing automobile pollutants has remained intact and states currently are required to meet standards for pollutants from stationary sources by Dec. 31, 1982. The Clean Air Amendments of 1977 set guidelines for "non-deterioration" of areas already in compliance with standards, and the 1974 Energy Supply Act extended deadlines for fuel-burning plants to provide for increased use of coal rather than oil.

At least as important as the clean air laws was the legislation to clean the nation's waters. The Water Quality Improvement Act of 1970 made petroleum companies liable for up to $14 million in oil-spill clean-up costs, strengthened restrictions on thermal pollution from nuclear power plants, ordered EPA to develop criteria covering the effects of pesticides in streams, rivers and other waters, and created an Office of Environmental Quality to act as staff for the Council on Environmental Quality. Still more comprehensive were the Water Pollution and Control Act Amendments of 1972, which set a national goal of eliminating all pollutant discharges into U.S. waters by 1985.[3]

The amendments required industries to use the "best practicable control technology currently available" by July 1, 1977, and the "best available technology economically achievable" by July 1, 1983. The amendments also authorized $24.6 billion to be spent on cleaning the nation's waters, including $18 billion in federal construction grants to states for building waste treatment plants.

The Resource Recovery Act of 1970 already had set up a modest program of demonstration and construction grants for innovative solid waste management systems.[4] In 1976, Congress passed the Resource Conservation and Recovery Act and the Toxic Substances Control Act, which gave EPA wide powers to set restrictions on disposal of toxic wastes and other hazardous substances. The Resource Conservation and Recovery Act set "cradle-to-grave" standards covering the generation and disposal of wastes, and the Toxic Substances Control Act required EPA to prepare guidelines for handling all toxic substances, with the exception of drugs, cosmetics and tobacco.[5]

Toting Up the Balance Sheet for a Decade

The National Wildlife Federation asserted in its tenth annual Environmental Quality Index, which it published early in 1979, that an "Environmental Revolution" comparable to the Industrial Revolution had taken place.[6] Not only did the decade produce "most of the basic legislation needed for environmental reform," but the public got "into decision-making at all levels of government" and "year after year, national opinion surveys constantly reveal[ed] a solid mass of public support for improved environmental quality." Because of that support, environmental arguments repeatedly "saved the day when the main issue seemed to be something else." The supersonic transport project, though economically dubious, was dropped mainly because of objections connected with noise, stratospheric pollu-

---

[3] See "Pollution Control: Costs and Benefits," *E.R.R.*, 1976 Vol. I, pp. 145-164.

[4] See "Solid Waste Technology," *E.R.R.*, 1974 Vol. II, pp. 641-664.

[5] See "Toxic Substance Control," *E.R.R.*, 1978 Vol. II, pp. 741-760.

[6] Gladwin Hill, "1969-1979: A Decade of Revolution," *National Wildlife*, February-March 1979, pp. 17-32.

tion, and fuel inefficiency; the Alaska pipeline project was drastically modified to meet environmental concerns; and the nation's nuclear power plant construction was sharply curtailed.[7]

Surveying the overall effects of environmentalist reform, however, the Wildlife Federation was rather more guarded in its enthusiasm. While a nationwide network of air-quality monitoring stations has been set up and even though 90 percent of the major U.S. factories are in compliance with pollution laws, the federation noted that most Americans continue to live in areas where the air is unsafe to breathe. "...[O]f the nation's 105 largest urban areas, only Honolulu has really clean air," and "smog remains a serious problem in nearly a fourth of the country's 3,200 counties."

NATIONAL ENVIRONMENTAL POLICY ACT OF 1969

P.L. 91-190, see page 950

Senate Report (Interior and Insular Affairs Committee) No. 91-296,
July 9, 1969 [To accompany S. 1075]

House September 23, December 22, 1969
No. 91-378, July 11, 19, 1969 [To accompany H.R. 12549]

Conference Report No. 91-765, Dec. 17, 1969
[To accompany S. 1075]

Cong. Record Vol. 115 (1969)

DATES OF CONSIDERATION AND PASSAGE

Senate July 10, December 20, 1969
House September 23, December 22, 1969

The Senate bill was passed in lieu of the House bill after substituting for its language much of the text of the House bill. The House Report and the Conference Report are set out.

HOUSE REPORT NO. 91-378

THE Committee on Merchant Marine and Fisheries, to whom was referred the bill (H.R. 12549), to amend the Fish and Wildlife Coordination Act to provide for the establishment of a Council on Environmental Quality, and for other purposes, having considered the same, report favorably thereon with an amendment and recommend that the bill as amended do pass.

PURPOSE OF THE BILL

The purpose of the bill, as hereby reported, is to create a Council on Environmental Quality with a broad and independent overview of current and long-term trends in the quality of our national environment, to ad-

Some 50 bodies of water, according to the Wildlife Federation, "have shown considerable improvement," and "about 3,600 of the nation's 4,000 major industrial polluters are meeting their clean-up deadlines." But the federation said scientists have been discovering new sources of water pollution faster than the known sources have been eliminated. In the matter of toxics, especially, the government has only just begun to assess the 10,000 landfill sites around the country "that have been used to get rid of up to 45 million tons of chemical wastes annually."

Because so many problems remain to be solved, environmentalists dearly hope to make as much progress in the Eighties as they did in the Seventies. A new consortium of national conservation groups, the Coast Alliance, plans to make 1980 the "Year of the Coasts." The alliance will encourage local groups to sponsor a variety of events and at the same time push for revision of federal laws affecting America's coastlines.[8]

Another group, the Citizens Committee for a Second Environmental Decade, plans to stage "Earth Day 80" on the tenth

---

[7] Congress in 1971 terminated federal support for the development of a commercial supersonic passenger transport (SST) plane, to compete with the British-French Concorde. For background, see Congressional Quarterly's *Congress and the Nation*, Vol. III, pp. 167-168. The Trans-Alaska Pipeline Authorization Act of 1973 overrode environmental objections to the construction of a pipeline from the North Slope to the ice-free port of Valdez, but by the time the line came into operation in 1977 the project had been substantially modified to meet environmental concerns.

[8] See "Making Waves," *Environmental Action,* September 1979, p. 4. See also "Coastal Zone Management," *E.R.R.,* 1976 Vol. II, pp. 863-882.

anniversary of the 1970 Earth Day to mobilize support for a renewed effort at improving the nation's quality of life. The Citizens Committee is a coalition of environmentalist leaders, national organizations and local groups. The emphasis is on local activitiy. Michael McCabe, executive director of Earth Day 80, said, "the most important legislation is complete at the national level, and the main task now will be implementation of laws and development of new issues."[9]

As former staff director of the Congressional Environmental Study Conference, an office which provides members of Congress with a weekly bulletin and background papers on legislative issues pertaining to the environment, McCabe does not completely discount prospects for continued legislative progress. From the time the study conference was founded in 1975, its membership has grown to include 72 senators and 245 representatives to become "the largest ad hoc organization in Congress."

Conflict With Energy Priority and Carter

According to estimates prepared by the Council on Environmental Quality, the nation as a whole — including both government and private industry — spent about $47.6 billion for pollution control in 1978.[10] Of that amount, less than half resulted from environmental legislation; but the CEQ estimates did not take into account the clean air and water pollution amendments of 1977 and the Resource Conservation and Toxic Substances Control Acts of 1976. When their costs are figured in, pollution abatement costs attributed to federal regulations go higher. The council projects the total costs resulting from federal laws at $361.3 billion for the years 1977 through 1986.

While the benefits of environmental regulation cannot easily be measured in dollars, almost everybody agrees that the costs will be increasingly hard to bear in a period of oil shortages, rampant inflation and economic recession. Because of such economic constraints, the political environment already is becoming more inhospitable to environmentalism, and one result has been a drastic change in President Carter's standing among environmentalists.

Carter appealed strongly to the environmentalists during his 1976 campaign, and during his first two years in office received high marks from them. At a press conference held in Washington on Dec. 20, 1978, over 30 environmentalist leaders gave Carter an "outstanding" rating for his performance, noting especially his efforts to protect Alaska wilderness, the high quality of

---

[9] Interview, Oct. 30, 1979. *Environmental Action,* which was founded by organizers of the first Earth Day, plans to support Earth Day 80 by encouraging the some 6,000 local groups with which it maintains contacts to stage events.

[10] Council on Environmental Quality, *Annual Report: 1978,* pp. 424, 428.

his appointments to environmental positions, and his attempts to block water projects they considered wasteful.[11] Environmentalists already had begun to worry, though, about remarks some administration officials were making about the necessity of assessing the inflationary impact of environmental regulation.

By the summer of 1979 the honeymoon was over. Carter sorely strained his relations with environmentalists on two occasions. First, on July 15 in a televised speech to the nation about energy needs, he said: "We will protect the environment. But if the nation needs to build a pipeline or a refinery — we will build them." In the days following the speech, Carter spelled out plans for an $88-billion synthetic fuels program and the creation of an Energy Mobilization Board with authority to bypass environmental standards.[12] Second, on Sept. 25 Carter signed into law a bill directing completion of the Tellico Dam in Tennessee.

The controversy over Tellico turned on the danger it posed to an endangered species, the tiny snail darter, which came to symbolize for environmentalists the broader threat that Congress would increasingly waive existing legislation for the sake of expediting priority projects. When Carter signed the bill exempting Tellico from all existing restrictions in federal law, the League of Conservation Voters sharply criticized his leadership, saying he lacked the nerve to stand up to Congress. Brock Evans, director of the Sierra Club's Washington office, said the president had "sent a clear message to anybody who worries about laws that stand in the way of pork barrel projects — 'don't worry about my views, I won't veto them.' "[13]

In decrying Carter's apostasy, environmentalists cite public opinion polls which continue to indicate — despite the country's economic problems — support for higher spending on pollution abatement.[14] *Audubon* magazine noted more sympathetically that Tellico was a hard decision for Carter to make. "His heart said veto. But practical politics said yes."[15] Many environmentalists recognize that the tide may be turning against them and that the environmental decade may be, in hindsight, just that — *the* environmental decade.

---

[11] In 1977 Carter tried to stop the federal financing of 19 water projects (dams, canals, etc.) as environmentally unsound and economically wasteful. Conservationists were delighted, but his plan met with stiff opposition in Congress and had to be substantially modified.

[12] See "Synthetic Fuels," *E.R.R.*, 1979 Vol. II, pp. 621-640. On Oct. 4. the Senate agreed to create an Energy Mobilization Board that could waive certain procedural requirements in order to expedite priority energy projects. On Nov. 1, the House agreed to a separate bill that would let the board waive certain substantive laws as well, with the permission of the president and both houses of Congress. The two versions of the Mobilization Board legislation now go to House-Senate conference to work out differences.

[13] Quoted in *The Washington Star*, Sept. 27, 1979.

[14] See for example Robert Cameron Mitchell, "Silent Spring — Solid Majorities," *Public Opinion*, August-September 1979, pp. 16-20.

[15] Robert Cahn, "Perspective: The Triumph of Wrong," *Audubon*, November 1979, p. 12.

Origins of Environmentalism

ENVIRONMENTALISM has roots going back more than a century, but the modern environmental movement as we know it today is of recent vintage, so recent that dictionaries have failed to keep pace with the concept. The 1977 edition of Webster's *New Collegiate Dictionary* defines environmentalism as "a theory that views environment rather than heredity as the important factor in the development and especially the cultural and intellectual development of an individual." This definition altogether misses the concern for the protection of nature that is at the heart of modern environmentalism, and it contains a view of heredity that few people would defend today.

Webster's definition seems to refer to the views espoused by some enlightenment philosophers in the 18th century, who thought that the environment completely determined human nature, and who believed that by perfecting the environment one could also perfect mankind. But modern environmentalists fear that it is precisely man's efforts to manipulate the environment which may be undermining the natural relationships that sustain all life on earth. In sharp contrast to the 18th century philosophers, modern environmentalists view life as a delicate balance of genetic and environmental factors, which is understood only partially and manipulated at mankind's peril.

Modern environmentalism, in fact, is rooted not so much in the 18th century as in the 19th century. Two developments account for its emergence. One was the publication in 1859 of Charles Darwin's *Origin of the Species,* which inspired systematic scientific research into the question of how groups of organisms adapt to their habitats. The other was the industrial revolution. By the end of the 1800s, squalid manufacturing cities, belching locomotives, and abysmal mining centers blighted the landscape and, often, the lives of the people.

Darwin advanced the theory in the *Origin of the Species* that evolution results from a process he called natural selection, or "survival of the fittest." Changes in individual organisms occur spontaneously as the result of hereditary factors, he said, and those organisms with the characteristics most suitable for their habitats survive. In Darwin's theory, which virtually all scientists now accept, evolution is equally the product of hereditary and environmental factors.

Publication of the *Origin of the Species* soon led to the creation of a new scientific field called "ecology." In 1869, the German biologist Ernst Haeckel stated that the individual was a product of cooperation between the environment and organismal

30

heredity. He termed this relationship "oecology," a word derived from the Greek meaning "house," and indicating the study of organisms in their natural environments. In the 1890s, ecology "was placed on a modern basis, more or less," by scientists working in Switzerland, Denmark and the United States. "Thereafter, research in ecological subjects tended to stress population and community analysis."[16]

Coincidentally, it was also in the 1890s that the first conservationist and naturalist social movements appeared. By then the industrial revolution was firmly entrenched in England, and the new industrial city of Manchester had become the world's leading symbol of all that industrialization meant — both good and bad. On the one hand, the Manchester School of political and economic liberalism, led by Richard Cobden and John Bright, maintained that absolutely free trade and unrestricted competition would lead to universal prosperity and world peace. On the other hand, critics of the industrial revolution from the political far left to the far right held that Manchester epitomized all that was dehumanizing about industrialization.

In Germany, where social critics were able to observe economic and political developments in England and France before they took hold in the "Fatherland," Manchester became a particularly potent symbol of what the future held in store. On the left, Karl Marx, working in collaboration with Friedrich Engels, the heir to a Manchester textile firm founded by his father, made Manchester a case study in his critique of industrial capitalism. On the right, numerous writers frequently invoked Manchester's squalor as an example of what "decadent bourgeois liberalism" would inevitably lead to.

It was in Germany where a sort of "back to the land" youth movement first developed, and around the turn of the century it became a firmly established social custom for adolescents to spend a year or two wandering about in natural surroundings before settling down.[17] Vulgarized Darwinian ideas connected with a cult of physical strength and racial purity had some play in the German youth movement, and they became an important ideological element in Hitler's imperialistic policies in Eastern Europe: his "push to the East" in search of *Lebensraum* — living space — for the German people.

Reformist Roots of American Environmentalism

In the United States industrialization proceeded in the late 19th century closely in tandem with Germany's economic development, and here too the first conservationist social movements

---

[16] Thomas Park, "Ecology," *Encyclopaedia Britannica* (1973), Vol. 7, p. 913. Park is a former president of the American Association for the Advancement of Science.

[17] See Walter Z. Laqueur, *Young Germany* (1962), p. 15.

emerged in the 1890s in response to fears that industrial squalor soon would destroy all remaining wilderness. But in the United States conservationism took hold with an especially strong grip, apparently because the first boom period of industrial capitalism coincided with the closing of the frontier. In 1890, as Frederick Jackson Turner pointed out on the first page of his famous essay on "The Significance of the Frontier in American History," the superintendent of the census announced that "there can hardly be said to be a frontier line" and that the frontier therefore could no longer "have a place in the census reports."[18] The closing of the frontier meant, among other things, that industry now would expand in a confined space and that individuals no longer would be able to escape industrialization simply by moving West.

On June 4, 1892, a group of people inspired by the naturalist-writer John Muir drew up the articles of incorporation for the Sierra Club. Many of these people were San Francisco professionals, and what they had in common was a love for the Yosemite Valley, which they wanted to protect from commercial exploitation. Meanwhile, on the other side of the continent, the first Audubon societies were founded in Massachusetts and Pennsylvania. Their main objective was to save bird and mammal species from extinction at the hands of plume hunters for the millinery trade and other commercial interests. Between 1895 and 1905 the first Audubon groups persuaded 32 states to enact bird protection laws, and in 1905 the groups incorporated in New York City as a national association.

The emergence of industrial capitalism and the closing of the frontier bred, in addition to conservationist movements, mounting concern about the deteriorating urban environment and the increasing monopolization of public resources. Muckrakers such as Lincoln Steffens (*The Shame of the Cities,* 1904), Ida Tarbell (*History of Standard Oil,* 1904), and Upton Sinclair (*The Jungle,* 1906), drew attention to the perils associated with unbridled industrial growth, not only in their books but also in a series of influential magazines such as *McClure's* and *Collier's.*

These reformers, Turner said, were "sounding the warning that American democratic ideals and society are menaced . . . by the very conditions that make this apparent prosperity; that the economic resources are no longer limitless and free; that the aggregate national wealth is increasing at the cost of present social justice and moral health, and the future well-being of the American people. The Granger and the Populist were prophets of this reform movement. Mr. [William Jennings] Bryan's

---

[18] Quoted by Frederick Jackson Turner in his book *The Frontier in American History* (1921), p. 1.

Democracy, Mr. [Eugene Victor] Debs' Socialism, and Mr. [Theodore] Roosevelt's Republicanism all had in common the emphasis upon the need of governmental regulation of industrial tendencies in the interest of the common man. . . ."[19]

As president from 1901 to 1909, Theodore Roosevelt conducted constant battles with the great trusts and combinations, and he saved extensive areas of the public domain from exploitation by private interests. He also was the first president to call attention to the problem of resource scarcity: In 1907 he summoned the governors of 46 states to ponder the danger of exhausting the nation's natural resources. But Roosevelt had an ambivalent relationship with the reformers, whom he was the first to call "muckrakers," referring to the Muck-raker in John Bunyan's *Pilgrim's Progress* who was so concerned with raking filth that he could not see the celestial crown offered him. And like other environmentalists after him, Roosevelt also was ambivalent about the closing of the frontier.[20]

New Knowledge About the Biological Chain

By World War I all major components of modern environmentalism had emerged: the science of ecology; conservationist and naturalist social movements; the critique of the urban and industrial environment created by unbridled industrial competition; and the concern about private exploitation of dwindling public resources. Why then did it take over 50 years for these strands to coalesce into a major national movement?

Part of the explanation would seem to be connected with a flood of external events that interrupted the development of environmentalism and had an especially disruptive effect on those who sought greater social control over the disposition of public resources. World War I, then the government raids against the political left in 1919, the unfettered capitalism of the 1920s, the Great Depression of the 1930s, World War II and finally the Cold War, each in turn created an inhospitable political atmosphere for doctrines of limited economic growth.

At the same time, some aspects of environmentalism, while very much alive, had yet to mature. The Sierra Club ceased to be merely a California organization and to acquire a national membership only in the 1940s. The Izaak Walton League and Wilderness Society were founded only in 1922 and 1935, respectively. The science of ecology, similarly, had a long way to go from being a mere concept to becoming a full-fledged research activity pursued by thousands of experts.

---

[19] *Ibid.*, p. 281.

[20] John F. Kennedy, similarly, was sympathetic to environmental concerns and campaigned with the slogan "The New Frontier" in 1960. Today, Gov. Edmund G. (Jerry) Brown Jr. of California espouses environmental concerns vigorously but also speaks frequently of outer space as America's new frontier.

Particularly important to the history of ecology were advances in population genetics, which researchers working in the United States, England and the Soviet Union developed into a precise mathematical science during the 1910s and 1920s. By the 1930s and 1940s, according to science historian Garland Allen, there was an "increasing realization that all biological phenomena are interconnected and could be dealt with in similar terms." Those terms were largely derived from genetics, Allen said, but they were applied in a new context, namely, "of the organism or population as an entity, a reacting system meaningful only in the context of its environmental surroundings."[21]

The advances in population genetics, and the development of increasingly refined techniques for tracing chemical substances through the biological chain, helped stimulate more and more detailed research into the interaction of individual species with their habitats. This was true not only within America's growing university complex, but also among amateur naturalists, and within newly organized government agencies such as the Fish and Wildlife Service, which was established in 1940. The person who by all accounts did more than any other individual to stimulate the creation of the contemporary environmental movement, Rachel Carson, was intimately familiar with all these aspects of ecological research.

Rachel Carson's Profound Public Influence

Carson did graduate work in genetics at Johns Hopkins University and post-graduate work at the Marine Biological Laboratory in Woods Hole, Mass. She had a profound love of nature and also happened to be a writer of considerable ability. In 1936 she went to work for the U.S. Bureau of Fisheries, which later became part of the Fish and Wildlife Service, and she subsequently became writer, then editor, and finally editor-in-chief of the Wildlife Service's publications.

In 1951 Carson published *The Sea Around Us,* a book about marine ecology which not only met with high acclaim among professional scientists but also stayed on the best-seller lists for 86 weeks. During the late 1950s she became deeply concerned about the effects such persistent pesticides as DDT were having on the natural environment, and during the final years of her life, while she was dying of cancer, she devoted herself to studying the pesticide problem. That work led to the publication of *Silent Spring,* first in an abridged version in *The New Yorker* in June 1961, then as a book in 1962. The title reflects her portrayal of an environment so poisoned that eventually it would be left without the birds and insects that provide the sounds of spring.

The publication of *Silent Spring* provoked fierce attacks from

---

[21] Garland Allen, *Life Science in the Twentieth Century* (1975), p. 144.

interests that had a hand in the pesticide business. Velsicol Chemical Corp. tried to get Houghton Mifflin to drop publication, objecting that the book created the "false impression that all business is grasping and immoral" and that it would lead to reduced use of "agricultural chemicals in this country and in the countries of western Europe, so that our supply of food will be reduced to east-curtain parity [Soviet-bloc levels]."[22] When CBS did a television program on April 3, 1963, called "The Silent Spring of Rachel Carson," three of the program's five sponsors withdrew just days before it was to be broadcast.[23]

Despite such pressures, Carson's work came to the attention of President Kennedy, who happened to be a reader of *The New Yorker*. On May 15, 1963, his Science Advisory Committee's pesticide panel issued a report calling for "orderly reduction in the use of pesticides." Beginning nine years later with a ban on most DDT uses, several pesticides have been restricted.

Rachel Carson

While Carson was instrumental in demonstrating what decades of neglect and abuse had done to America's ecology, and while she showed that powerful vested interests could be defeated, most observers of environmentalism attribute the movement's coalescence in the late 1960s to a variety of other factors as well. In 1966, the first photos from outer space showed the entire globe and brought home to millions, as nothing ever had before, that human beings are one race confined to one geographic space. Then there were offshore oil spills that drew public attention.

Finally, a number of important changes were drastically altering the nation's social and political atmosphere. The civil rights and anti-war movements, together with the coming of age of the baby-boom generation, led to widespread questioning of authority of all kinds. At the same time, disillusionment with suburbia was beginning to manifest itself. Many people had fled the cities in the hope of living close to nature, and what many of them found instead were endless strings of superhighways, fast food chains and used car lots.[24]

---

[22] Quoted by Frank Graham Jr. in *Since Silent Spring* (1970), p. 49.

[23] They were Standard Brands and Ralston Purina, both major agribusiness concerns, and Lehn and Fink Products, manufacturer of Lysol.

[24] Gus Speth, chairman of the CEQ, stressed the importance of this last point in an interview, Oct. 29, 1979.

Changes in the Movement

THE COMBINATION of influences that came into play in the 1960s soon led to the foundation of numerous new environmental groups, many of which had objectives going far beyond traditional conservationist concerns. The controversy over persistent pesticides, for example, led to the creation of one of that decade's most influential organizations. In 1966 a New York lawyer, Victor Yannocone, brought suit against the Suffolk County (Long Island) Mosquito Control Commission on behalf of his wife, who was worried about the effects of local DDT spraying. Yannocone lost the suit, despite financial assistance from Audubon and technical advice from scientists at the Brookhaven National Laboratory and the State University of New York at Stony Brook, but the case inspired him to found the Environmental Defense Fund (EDF). As an organization combining scientists and lawyers, EDF went on to bring many successful suits on behalf of environmental interests.[25]

A similar organization, the Natural Resources Defense Council, was founded in 1970 by a group of students at Yale Law School. Inspired by the National Association for the Advancement of Colored People's Legal Defense Fund, the students wanted to advance environmental interests in the courts. The Ford Foundation became interested in the project and put the students in touch with a New York group, the Scenic Hudson Preservation Conference, which was fighting to block a hydroelectric project at Storm King Mountain along the Hudson River. Together the two groups formed the NRDC, and like the Environmental Defense Fund, NRDC brought many important and successful law suits in the Seventies.

A more purely scientific environmental organization, the Union of Concerned Scientists (UCS), was organized in 1969 by student activists at the Massachusetts Institute of Technology who wanted to take public positions on the misuse of technology — primarily in Vietnam and in the strategic arms race. Much of UCS's work soon came to be focused on the issue of nuclear safety, and some persons whom the organization backed — notably Dan Ford and Henry Kendall — became the nation's leading critics of the emergency core cooling system designed for nuclear power plants.

While groups like EDF, UCS and NRDC have their strongest roots in the scientific community, other groups founded in the Seventies hearken back to the Progressive and socialist traditions of muckrakers Ida Tarbell, Lincoln Steffens and Upton

[25] See Joel Primack and Frank von Hippel's *Advice and Dissent: Scientists in the Political Arena* (1974), pp. 128-142.

Sinclair. Environmental Action is a group best known for its "Dirty Dozen" campaign every two years to defeat 12 members of Congress selected for their anti-environment voting record. This organization emphasizes the urban environment along with more conventional ecological concerns such as bottle recycling and toxics. The Environmentalists for Full Employment, founded in 1976 with the support of about 100 sponsoring groups, works with labor, urban and environmental groups on issues of mutual concern. The Urban Environmental Conference, founded in 1971, is a coalition of organizations ranging from the National Urban League to the United Steel Workers.

As groups based in scientific and progressive political traditions have carved out a sizable role for themselves, the older conservationist organizations have responded to the challenge by broadening their concerns and by adopting the most modern political tactics. The Alaska Coalition, which has been urging the government since early in 1977 to set aside 170 million acres of Alaska as parks and refuges, represents the most impressive single effort that has been organized by conservationists. The coalition has employed computerized lists, phone banks, some 10,000 volunteers, and three separate professional staffs to work on grass-roots organizing, lobbying, and media relations.[26]

Criticism That Elitism, Anti-Science Prevail

Critics of environmentalism have accused the movement of promoting an irrational suspicion of science and technology, and of furthering the interests of a privileged few at the expense of the vast majority of ordinary Americans. "The talk of survival, limited resources and austerity does not crimp the lifestyle of suburban environmentalists, but only of the people they keep outside," asserts Bernard Frieden, a professor at the Massachusetts Institute of Technology.[27]

From its earliest days environmentalism has been vulnerable to pseudo-scientific ideas, and many of the early conservationists really were members of a social elite that could afford to enjoy the splendors of undisturbed nature. Most of the people who staff the leading environmental groups today are products of the nation's social and educational elite, and many of the people they claim to represent do indeed express an indiscriminate hostility to all things modern.

Even so, the critics of environmentalism may be somewhat undiscriminating, unable to discern its numerous strains — some scientific and some anti-scientific, some left-wing in their political orientation and some right-wing. Competition among

---

[26] See Gail Robinson's "The Lessons of the Alaska Coalition," *Environmental Action,* Sept. 23, 1978, pp. 10-11.

[27] Bernard Frieden, author of *The Environmental Protection Hustle* (1979), quoted in "Environmentalism: Assessing the Impact," *Energy Daily,* Aug. 2, 1979, p. 4.

the different approaches to environmentalism tends to keep the movement alert and self-critical, and as the Seventies have drawn to a close, fresh ideas and strong personalities have continued to breed new organizations representing varied constituencies.

One trend which many observers expect to become stronger in the Eighties is a preoccupation with technical issues. Whereas passage of legislation tended to be the goal in the Seventies, the emphasis in the Eighties is likely to be on carrying out existing laws. Local groups have a greater voice in how national objectives are met in specific situations, such as in state implementation plans required by clean air legislation. And several national organizations devote considerable attention to monitoring the activities of government agencies in a broad array of environmental fields. The Environmental Policy Center, for example, does highly regarded technical work on a wide range of issues.

EPC was founded in 1972 by people who had broken away from the Friends of the Earth, which itself was established in 1969 by David Brower shortly after he left the Sierra Club as executive director. FOE concentrates on global issues such as nuclear proliferation and world energy policy, typifying a trend in environmentalism at an opposite extreme from the technical and local issues which other groups prefer to work on. Many environmental problems — such as rising carbon dioxide levels, acid rain and global population growth — transcend national boundaries and can be solved only by means of cooperation among environmentalists working in many countries.

Friends of the Earth has branches in 22 countries, and some such as the British and French branches are highly influential. Other organizations such as Worldwatch in Washington, D.C., and The Institute for World Order in New York City specialize in a more scholarly approach to global issues, after the fashion of the peace research institutes which were set up decades ago in countries such as Sweden, Norway and Holland.[28]

Urban Environment and Financing in the 1980s

Another area likely to receive more attention is the urban environment. Most Americans, after all, live in urban areas. Rep. Joseph L. Fisher, D-Va., former president of Resources for the Future and the current co-chairman of the Environmental Study Conference, thinks that legislative efforts now "must go beyond pollution, toxics, and so forth, and take on the broader dimensions of the urban environment such as congestion." Fisher, who has served extensively on local planning boards in

---

[28] The best known of these is the Stockholm International Peace Research Institute, a leading independent authority on global military trends.

Virginia, believes that the broad problems can be solved only by means of long-range planning and that the federal government can do much to assist localities in improving their planning capabilities.[29]

Fisher, as a political moderate who approaches problems in a pragmatic fashion, hopes to prevent the 1980s from becoming a "period of confrontation between energy proponents and environmentalists." Many environmentalists are far less sanguine than Fisher about the effects of energy shortages and economic stagnation in the 1980s. To be sure, environmental regulation may have less harmful effects on employment than is generally imagined. Data Resources Inc., in a study completed in January 1979, estimated that in the period 1970-1986 the unemployment rate would be lower with pollution control expenditures than without.[30]

One direct effect of inflation and fears of a recession, however, is that contributions to environmental groups have slowed at a time their programs are expanding. In the case of the organizations that specialize in legal work, such as EDF and NRDC, a withdrawal of Ford Foundation money has compounded difficulties. While Ford had been expected to cut funding eventually, since the foundation has a policy of not financing projects in perpetuity, the cuts come at a time when it is exceptionally difficult to raise money from other sources.

But while some individual groups may go under in the 1980s, there is little doubt that environmentalism as a movement will survive a period of austerity. Gus Speth, chairman of the Council on Environmental Quality, comments: "People still have to care about the environment because it affects them in so many ways: oil spills, emphysema, cancer, recreation, food, resource questions. These problems are going to stay until they're solved."[31]

A major problem facing environmentalism in the 1980s is likely to be harmonization of internal differences, as the movement embraces more and more wide-ranging concerns. Environmentalists already are quite bitterly divided on some of the major policy issues of the day. Conservationist organizations tended to favor Carter's plan for oil-price decontrol, while groups aligned with urban, minority, and labor interests preferred rationing and stricter public regulation of the energy corporations. In the sensitive area of population policy, environmentalists are divided between those who would minimize

---

[29] Interview, Nov. 1, 1979.

[30] Study cited by Charles Doherty in "The Economic Impact of a Clean Environment," *The AFL-CIO American Federationist,* October 1979, pp. 3-4.

[31] Interview, Oct. 29, 1979.

any additional immigration into the United States and those who believe that this country should do more to relieve poor countries of their population pressures. A recent article in *Environmental Action* magazine advocating open immigration into the United States from Mexico touched off a storm of indignation among environmentalists.[32]

Environmentalists — like many of the species they try to protect — have displayed a formidable capacity for spontaneous change and growth in unexpected directions. But unlike many of the organisms that geneticists like to study in their natural habitats, environmentalists live in a global habitat which itself is changing rapidly in unpredictable directions. Any number of strains in environmentalism could prove suitable to the needs of the 1980s, and depending on how successful those strains are in competition with other emerging social trends, the Eighties may or may not be yet another environmental decade.

---

[32] See Rice Odell's "The Illegal Immigration Bugaboo," *Environmental Action*, June 1979, pp. 14-15, and November 1979, pp. 2-3, for responses.

Selected Bibliography

Books

Allen, Garland, *Life Science in the Twentieth Century*, John Wiley and Sons, 1975.

Carson, Rachel, *Silent Spring*, Houghton Mifflin Co., 1962.

Gilliam, Ann, ed., *Voices for the Earth: A Treasury of the Sierra Club Bulletin: 1893-1977*, Sierra Club Books, 1979.

Graham, Frank Jr., *Since Silent Spring*, Houghton Mifflin Co., 1970.

Nash, Roderick, ed., *The American Environment*, Wesley Publishing Co., 1976.

Primack, Joel and Frank von Hippel, *Advice and Dissent: Scientists in the Political Arena*, Basic Books, Inc., 1974.

Articles

Audubon, selected issues.

Environmental Action, selected issues.

National Wildlife, selected Issues.

Sierra Club Bulletin, selected issues.

White, Lynn Jr., "The Ecology of Our Science," *Science 80*, November-December 1979, pp. 72-76.

Reports and Studies

Council on Environmental Quality, *Environmental Quality*, 9th annual report, Washington, D.C., 1978.

Editorial Research Reports: "Environmental Policy," 1974 Vol. II, p. 945; "Pollution Control: Costs and Benefits," 1976 Vol. I, p. 145; "Toxic Substance Control," 1978 Vol. II, p. 741.

AMERICA'S CHANGING WORK ETHIC

by

Sandra Stencel

Dec. 14
1 9 7 9

AMERICA'S CHANGING WORK ETHIC

HOW MANY people work in your organization?" one executive asked another. "About half." This old joke still is repeated in corporate boardrooms across the nation, but it probably produces fewer chuckles today than it did in the past. Growing concern about the United States' relatively sluggish productivity record of recent years has made worker performance a topic of intense scrutiny and debate. President Carter, in a televised address to the nation July 15, singled out declining productivity as one of the symptoms of the "crisis of the American spirit" which he said was "threatening to destroy the social and political fabric of America."

Many economists and business executives regard productivity, broadly defined as output per man-hour, as the best single measure of the economy's vitality. Certainly it is the most complex economic indicator, reflecting the contribution not only of labor but also of technology, managerial expertise, wealth and natural resources. From the end of World War II through the 1960s, productivity in the United States rose by slightly more than 3 percent a year, reaching a peak around 1966. The rate of increase has slowed down since then; in 1978 it was only 0.4 percent. During the first nine months of 1979, the productivity rate actually declined,[1] making it likely that the nation will post a decline for the year as a whole. In the 32 years the U.S. government has been keeping records on productivity it has dropped only once — in 1974, at the start of the country's steepest postwar recession.

Improving America's productivity will not be easy, since numerous factors have contributed to its decline. But most business leaders and economists agree that without workers' support, the task will be nearly impossible. "As the American economy becomes more labor-intensive as a result of the shift towards service, clerical and knowledge work," James J. O'Toole, associate professor of management at the University of Southern California Graduate School of Business, wrote recently, "the attitudes of workers become central factors in national productivity."[2]

---

[1] By 3 percent, at an annual rate, during the first quarter, by 2.2 percent in the second quarter and by 0.7 percent in the third quarter.

[2] James J. O'Toole, "Dystopia: The Irresponsible Society," *Management Review*, October 1979, p. 12. *Management Review* is published by American Management Associations. O'Toole served as a special assistant to the Secretary of Health, Education and Welfare during the Nixon administration and was chairman of the Secretary's Special Task Force on Work in America see p. 46)

While there are differences of opinion about whether changes in worker attitudes have affected U.S. productivity *(see p. 50)*, there seems to be general agreement that a new work ethic has evolved. The feelings of many workers, no doubt, were expressed in a recent popular song by Johnny Paycheck, "Take This Job and Shove It!" According to labor analyst John R. Browning, contemporary workers do not view their jobs as a simple contract — a day's work for a day's pay. "Today's workers want much more," he said recently. "They want nothing less than eight hours of meaningful, skillfully guided, personally satisfying work for eight hours pay. And that's not easy for most companies to provide."[3]

Pollster Daniel Yankelovich says that today's "new breed" workers "have come to feel that success is not enough to satisfy their yearnings for self-fulfillment. They are reaching out for something different. . . . Somehow the conventional systems no longer satisfy their deepest psychological needs nor nourish their self-esteem, nor fulfill their cravings for the 'full, rich life.' "[4] Similar sentiments were expressed recently by William M. Batten, chairman of the New York Stock Exchange. "Better education and training have reshaped and redirected people's requirements and expectations," Batten said Nov. 26 in a lecture at the Wharton School of the University of Pennsylvania. "A stronger sense of self-worth and greater assertiveness and self-confidence inevitably have prompted searching questions about the values of the past. Changes in social climate and a growing insistence on individual rights have given new dimensions to such concepts as human dignity and equal opportunity."

Batten, however, criticized the tendency to equate changing attitudes toward work with the death of the work ethic. "There is a very great difference between not wanting to work and being dissatisfied with the particular job you happen to be working at," he said. "Perhaps the biggest problem today is to reorganize work in ways that will enable workers to derive satisfaction from it."

The link between worker attitudes and productivity has been a source of mounting concern since the early 1970s.[5] In 1973 the National Commission on Productivity commissioned a national survey to find out what workers thought about efforts to increase productivity. Only 20 percent of the respondents felt that employees "benefitted a lot" from increased productivity. The commission noted: "While there is unanimity among economists and policymakers that productivity growth is the key to our eco-

---

[3] Quoted in *U.S. News & World Report,* Sept. 3, 1979, p. 35.
[4] Quoted by Bernard Lefkowitz in *Breaktime: Living Without Work in a Nine to Five World* (1979), p. 14.
[5] See "Productivity and the New Work Ethic," *E.R.R.,* 1972 Vol. I, pp. 291-310.

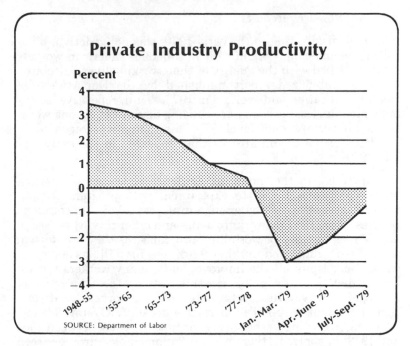

Private Industry Productivity

Percent

SOURCE: Department of Labor

nomic strength — the source of jobs and prosperity — most Americans . . . believe it is not they, the wage earners, who benefit from productivity gains, but rather stockholders or those who receive the profits generated by productivity growth. . . . Exhortations on the value of hard work do little to improve public understanding of the importance of productivity increases to national growth and often add to the atmosphere of mistrust."[6]

Signs of Widespread Job Dissatisfaction

Most discussions of worker discontent in the early 1970s centered on blue-collar workers.[7] An article in the July 1970 issue of *Fortune* described "the deep dislike of the job and the desire to escape" among production workers in automobile plants. This was shown in high rates of absenteeism, tardiness, turnover and discipline problems. "In their present temper," the author wrote, they "would probably like nothing better than to down tools for a rousing great strike."[8] That's just what workers did two years later at the General Motors complex at Lordstown, Ohio. The workers struck for 22 days in March 1972 protesting new methods intended to make the assembly line more efficient. Russell W. Gibbons, a labor editor writing in *Commonweal*, called the Lordstown strike "the most dramatic instance of worker resistance since the Flint sit-downs in 1937."[9]

---

[6] "Second Annual Report of the National Commission on Productivity," 1973, p. xix. The commission was set up by President Nixon in 1970.
[7] See "Blue-Collar America," *E.R.R.*, 1970 Vol. II, pp. 627-646.
[8] Judson Gooding, "Blue-Collar Blues on the Assembly Line," *Fortune*, July 1970, p. 71.
[9] Russell W. Gibbons, "Showdown at Lordstown," *Commonweal*, March 3, 1972, p. 523.

Worker disaffection in the early 1970s was not strictly a blue-collar phenomenon. "Significant numbers of American workers are dissatisfied with the quality of their working lives," declared a widely publicized report published by the Department of Health, Education and Welfare in 1973. "Dull, repetitive, seemingly meaningless tasks . . . are causing discontent among workers at all occupational levels."[10] This theme was repeated in hundreds of books and articles that appeared in the early and mid-1970s.[11]

Responding to the mounting evidence of worker alienation, many companies began to experiment with programs to humanize the work place by giving employees a voice in company policies, more flexible working hours and other privileges *(see p. 55)*. These "quality of work life" programs, as they are known, undoubtedly improved working conditions for millions of Americans. But despite all the improvements, many workers remain dissatisfied. A study published this year by the University of Michigan's Survey Research Center showed worker dissatisfaction at the highest point in at least a decade.[12] Overall job satisfaction, according to the survey, dropped slightly between 1967 and 1973; in contrast, there was an "appreciable" drop between 1973 and 1977. "The decline in job satisfaction has been pervasive, affecting virtually all demographic and occupational classes," the researchers reported.

A portrait of deepening discontent among American workers also emerged from a recent analysis of employee attitude data gathered over a 27-year period (1950-1977) by Opinion Research Corporation of Princeton, N.J. "While companies seem to be doing more now than they were during the 1950s, what they are doing today is simply not viewed by employees as acceptable," the researchers said in an article in *Harvard Business Review*. "As employees have become more educated and have developed new values, their expectations for responsiveness from their companies have changed."[13]

Not surprisingly, the Princeton group found that managers usually are more satisfied than are clerical and hourly employees. Clerical workers' job satisfaction declined 10 percent between 1970 and 1977, while hourly workers' job satisfaction

---

[10] *Work in America: Report of the Special Task Force of the Secretary of Health, Education and Welfare* (1973).

[11] See, for example, Jerome M. Rosow, ed., *The Worker and the Job: Coping with Change* (1974); Harold Sheppard and Neal Herrick, *Where Have All the Robots Gone?* (1972); Sar A. Levitan and William B. Johnston, *Work Is Here To Stay, Alas* (1973); and Irving Howe, ed., *The World of the Blue-Collar Worker* (1972).

[12] See Graham L. Staines and Robert P. Quinn, "American Workers Evaluate the Quality of Their Jobs," *Monthly Labor Review*, January 1979, pp. 3-12 and Graham L. Staines, "Is Worker Dissatisfaction Rising?" *Challenge*, May-June 1979, pp. 38-44.

[13] M. R. Cooper, B. S. Morgan, P. M. Foley and L. B. Kaplan, "Changing Employee Values: Deepening Discontent?" *Harvard Business Review*, January-February 1979, pp. 117-125.

dropped over 5 percent. During the same period, managers' ratings of their job satisfaction stayed about the same. Satisfaction with salaries has substantially increased among all three groups of employees, despite continuing concern about inflation and the resulting decline in purchasing power. "However, hourly and clerical employees' satisfaction with pay does not offset either their high level of job dissatisfaction or their feeling that they are not treated with respect as individuals," the researchers said. Dissatisfaction among hourly and clerical workers, they concluded, "is every bit as pervasive" as dissent on college campuses in the late 1960s and "seems to be growing."

Discontent Among White-Collar Employees

One indication of the intensity of feeling among clerical employees is the growing interest in unionization of female office workers — whom union leaders long had considered too difficult to organize. On the West Coast, office workers in the movie business are pushing to be included in industry-wide contract negotiations for the first time. At Boston University, clerical and library workers have organized and are negotiating contracts. The Teamsters union successfully organized the 1,900 clerical workers at the University of Chicago.

Most of the recent attempts to organize clerical workers have come from outside the traditional union framework. For example, a drive to upgrade salaries and promotional opportunities in banks has been organized by a network of 13 organizations loosely affiliated as the National Association of Working Women. According to Karen Nussbaum, head of the association, about 1.25 million of the nation's 2 million bank employees are women, and 85 percent are in low-paying clerical jobs.

The possibilities of using the independent women's groups, which can reach many women who might initially be turned off by a traditional union, have recently been recognized by at least one major union. The 550,000-member Communications Workers of America (AFL-CIO) has started a program with a Chicago group called Women Employed. The group will do the ground work in organizing a number of work places, turning over to the union information on successful techniques and the names of women who may be interested in an organizing drive.

The Communications Workers would then take responsibility for the organization drive itself. The union recently allocated funds to expand the project to include other working women's groups around the country. "I don't know of any union that has really tried to get at these workers," said Patsy Fryman, assistant to CWA President Watts, "but we are sure going to try."[14]

---

[14] Quoted in *The New York Times*, July 9, 1979.

Last spring the Communications Workers of America launched a campaign to combat job stress among the half-million workers employed by the Bell Telephone System. Targets of the union's ire include compulsory overtime, arbitrary absenteeism controls and computerized scheduling so exacting that it results in what the union derisively calls "timed potty breaks." To dramatize their complaints, telephone workers last June 15 staged demonstrations in cities around the country. "Although white-collar workers are likelier to work in cleaner surroundings than their co-workers in the factory. . . ," Watts said, "they often find themselves reduced by automation to tasks that are just as monotonous. . . ."[15]

Youth and the Psychology of 'Entitlement'

Many social observers view the changing attitudes toward work as an outgrowth of the "psychology of entitlement." "Workers have an expanding sense of what is due them as *rights* of employment or citizenship," wrote James J. O'Toole. "From pensions to health care, to long vacations, to a high standard of living, the perception by workers of what constitutes their rights is inexorably being enlarged."

Such attitudes usually are attributed to the so-called "permissive" generation of the late 1940s and 1950s. *Time* magazine described them as "part of the instant-gratification, self-indulgent 'Me Decade,' with a taste for high-priced living and little interest in self-denial."[16] Many managers say that younger workers are more apt than their older counterparts to reject transfers, decline promotions, switch jobs or refuse to work overtime for personal reasons. With a growing number of two-income families,[17] workers also are demanding more time off from the job. Some need the free time for child-rearing responsibilities. Others simply have more money to spend on leisure activities.

Chester A. Morgan, a labor economics professor at the University of Iowa, argues that much of the criticism directed at today's young workers is the same sort of fault-finding that the older generation has always directed toward the younger. If a diminution in both enthusiasm and skills has occurred, Morgan goes on to say, perhaps it is not entirely the fault of the young. This generation was plagued "by the curse of affluence," he wrote. "Their parents had experienced the depression and deprivations of the 1930s and were determined their children should not go through the same experience. Consequently most didn't. . . ."[18] According to Fordham University Professors Su-

---

[15] Quoted in *The Washington Post*, May 29, 1979.

[16] *Time*, May 28, 1978, p. 39.

[17] See "Two-Income Families," *E.R.R.*, 1979 Vol. II, pp. 501-520.

[18] Chester A. Morgan, "Up With Young Employees," *Business Horizons*, October 1978, pp. 47-48.

Employee Rights

"Issues of employee rights are going to be as central for corporate management in the 1980s as equal employment opportunity became in the 1960s and 1970s," according to Xerox chairman Peter McCulloch. American workers already are taking their bosses to court to challenge everything from dress codes to the use of their personnel files. The American Civil Liberties Union reports that its biggest case load now involves worker complaints against employers. Case loads also have soared at federal agencies that hear employee complaints about occupational health and safety, discrimination and wage-and-hour violations.

Over 200 corporate executives and civil liberties' advocates attended a two-day Seminar on Individual Rights in the Corporation, held last June in New York. The principal topic of conversation was employee privacy. A recent Louis Harris Survey of public and employee attitudes about privacy indicated that 64 percent of the people feel a "sense of real concern" about threats to their personal privacy. The survey, sponsored by Sentry Insurance, found that by a large majority employees want legislation outlawing the use of lie detectors in hiring, use of closed-circuit television to check worker efficiency and monitoring of employee conversations to learn what they think about supervisors and managers.

Many also want a ban on asking job applicants to take psychological tests. Some 70 percent of the employees polled want access to personnel files, including medical records, and 83 percent thought it was very important to notify an employee before releasing any information from his or her employment files. "Taken in the aggregate," said Louis Harris, these and other viewpoints expressed in the poll "add up to the demand for a new employee bill of rights in business and government."

san Gray and Louis Henri Bolce, "the affluence and success of their parents exact another toll from the success/work ethic by making it difficult for a middle-class youth to . . . better himself materially over his parents. . . . He therefore sees himself condemned as a failure relative to his parents [and is] likely to be susceptible to the ideology that repudiates the value of striving to get ahead. . . ."[19]

Gail Sheehy, the author of *Passages: Predictable Crises of Adult Life* (1976), had another explanation for today's "laidback" philosophy. "Following their fathers' route to happiness is seen by many younger men as a fate marginally better than early suicide," she wrote in a recent article in *Esquire* magazine. "They dread waking up at the age of 55 from the money-power-fame-success grind they watched their fathers pursue to find they have only a few years left to enjoy life between the first and the final heart attacks."[20]

---

[19] Quoted in *Breaktime, op. cit.*, p. 49.
[20] Gail Sheehy, "Introducing the Postponing Generation: The Truth About Today's Young Men," *Esquire*, October 1979, p. 25.

Impact on U.S. Productivity

I S THE weakening of productivity growth in the United States a result of a deterioration in attitudes toward work? According to Edward F. Denison, a leading authority on productivity, "this is without doubt the number one popular explanation of low productivity."[21] The comments of Thomas A. Murphy, chairman of the General Motors Corp., are typical: "Our national production rate has fallen behind those of other countries because many of them are prepared to make greater sacrifices than we are. The workers of Japan, for instance, are motivated by a relentless work ethic. As a nation, they are prepared to work harder — and even cut corners — to keep goods flowing abroad."[22]

Those who share Murphy's views include Arthur F. Burns, former chairman of the Federal Reserve Board. "A substantial part" of the recent productivity slowdown in the United States could be explained by "a lessened sense of industriousness on the part of our work force," Burns told a college graduating class in 1977.

> It is not at all clear [Burns continued] that people actually perceive that lessened work effort inevitably must be reflected in the material benefits we as a people can enjoy. That linkage was inescapably evident earlier in our history — when, to a much greater degree than is now the case, men and women could literally see what their individual effort yielded in consumable products; but the linkage has been blurred as our productive and distributive mechanisms have grown in complexity.[23]

Most economists downplay the human element in the productivity problem. Denison wrote: "I am skeptical that a sudden drop in willingness to work is responsible for the recent retardation of productivity. . . . My skepticism is largely attributable to having heard similar generalizations all my life and having read them in the works of observers who wrote long before my birth. . . . These generalizations, moreover, are also common in other countries, including those with excellent records for raising productivity." Similar comments were expressed recently by Secretary of Labor F. Ray Marshall. "Let's not blame people for our declining productivity," Marshall said.

---

[21] Edward F. Denison, "Explanations of Declining Productivity Growth," *Survey of Current Business,* August 1979, p. 13. Denison is associate director of the Bureau of Economic Analysis of the U.S. Department of Commerce and senior fellow emeritus of the Brookings Institution.

[22] Quoted by Milton Rockmore in "Why U.S. Lags: A Symposium By the Experts," *Parade,* Nov. 25, 1979, p. 27.

[23] Commencement address at the University of South Carolina, May 14, 1977, on "The Significance of Our Productivity Lag."

"The willingness to work is rarely correlated with high productivity.... The problem is more often in the system."[24]

Other Explanations for Growth Slowdown

Many attribute part of the slowdown to the passing of an era in which major productivity gains were realized as a result of the shift of a significant portion of the population out of agriculture into rapidly expanding manufacturing industries. Some experts hypothesize that the more recent growth of the service sector has caused some decline in productivity because labor-intensive services are unlikely to have as high a productivity rate as manufacturing. Some economists also believe that the influx of the postwar "baby-boom" generation and large numbers of women into the labor force have pulled down the productivity rate. Young and inexperienced workers normally are less productive than others.

One of the most important factors influencing productivity is technological change. Most experts agree that the United States has lost much of the technological superiority it enjoyed immediately after World War II. Explanations of the causes vary. The conclusions of a two-day meeting held by the American Association for the Advancement of Science in June 1978 were summarized in *The Washington Post* as follows: "The United States is losing its competitive edge in technology because American industry is spending less on research and because the federal government withdrew much of its support for industrial research at the ends of the Apollo space program and the Vietnam War." If expressed as a percentage of gross national product (GNP), total spending for research and development in the United States rose from 0.95 in 1955 to a peak of 2.97 in 1964, then slipped gradually to 2.27 in 1976 and 1977 and 2.2 in 1978.

The postwar jump in productivity is attributed by some to a wave of new advances in knowledge made possible by science-based technology. In their view this wave has passed. This opinion is often based on reasoning such as that of Orio Giarini, who stated that "we are more and more coming to the point where science-based technology, at least in certain sectors, has exploited all the major possibilities made available by the scientific advances of the last century," and that we may have to wait decades for the reservoir to be replenished.[25]

A recent publication of the Morgan Guaranty Trust Co. stated that "the single most important cause" of the U.S. productivity

---

[24] Quoted in *Parade*, p. 27.

[25] Orio Giarini, "Economics, Vulnerability and the Diminishing Returns of Technology," *The Geneva Papers on Risk and Insurance*, No. 6 (October 1977), p. 10, quoted in Denison, *op. cit.*, p. 8. Giarini is secretary general of the International Association for Risk and Insurance Economics Research.

slowdown is "the low level of capital investment in recent years with consequent slow growth of the capital stock."

> Over the decades prior to the 1970s [the article stated], the capital available to each worker rose significantly. For example, between 1948 and 1969 the ratio between the capital stock and the total number of man-hours worked (the capital-labor ratio) almost doubled. . . . To be sure, there were other important contributing factors to productivity growth (such as technological innovations and improvements in the quality of the labor force), but a rising capital-labor ratio has been a major and, until recently, steady spur to productivity improvement.[26]

The low level of investment in the United States is not well understood. Until recently experts believed that the 1974-75 recession left many industries saddled with excess manufacturing capacity. With a lot of plant and equipment lying idle, there was little reason to invest in expansion or improvements. William Bowen wrote recently in *Fortune* magazine that "the sluggishness in capital spending can be largely explained as a consequence of the resurgence of inflation after the 1974-75 recession. . . . Among other things [inflation] pushes up interest rates, worsens perceived risk-reward ratios and shortens time horizons."[27]

Some argue that the key factor discouraging investment has been low corporate profits. By most measures, profits have been lower through the 1970s than they were in the 1950s and 1960s when investment was quite strong. According to Sen. Jacob K. Javits, R-N.Y., low corporate profits are both a result and a cause of inflation. "The stagnation of productivity is such a vicious cycle," he said. "Inflation lowers real profits, which leads to reduced investment, which, in turn, is responsible for stagnant productivity, which further worsens inflation."[28]

"A far from minor influence on productivity growth since 1966 has been the increase in burdens imposed on business by federal regulation," Bowen said in *Fortune*. Government rules have forced companies to spend more money on environmental quality and occupational health and safety. However, the output from those investments — clean air, longer and healthier lives, and so on — is not included in productivity calculations. The Denison study concluded that the direct costs of complying with environmental, health and safety regulations may have reduced annual productivity growth by 0.3 percentage points from 1973 to 1976. The flood of paperwork necessary to comply with gov-

---

[26] "Investment and the Growth of Productivity," *The Morgan Guaranty Survey*, September 1979, pp. 10-11.

[27] William Bowen, "Better Prospects for Our Ailing Productivity," *Fortune*, Dec. 3, 1979, p. 74.

[28] Quoted in *Congressional Quarterly Weekly Report*, June 16, 1979, p. 1156.

ernment regulations also absorbs resources and time that could otherwise be used to produce measured output. The Federal Commission on Paperwork, in its final report issued in January 1978, estimated that the paperwork necessary to meet federal requirements cost American businesses $25 billion to $32 billion in 1976.[29]

Many experts agree that rising energy costs have hurt productivity, although the actual effects are difficult to quantify. High energy costs have forced a number of industries to invest funds in energy purchases and conservation, rather than for basic research and development that might improve productivity. Some also believe that the high cost of energy has led some industries to substitute labor for more efficient but energy-consuming equipment. While that may have helped bring the unemployment rate down, it has probably slowed productivity improvements.

Comparisons With Western Europe, Japan

Comptroller General Elmer B. Staats has observed that various institutions cooperate much more closely in efforts to improve productivity in Western Europe and Japan than they do in the United States. "Other countries are sustaining higher rates of productive growth," he said, "because they have found ways to achieve close harmony among institutions necessary to technology development — government, finance and industry and the universities. But in the United States, many perceive an almost adversary relationship among these elements."[30]

The United States still outproduces its foreign competitors, but the gap is closing. It took seven Japanese workers to produce as much as one American in 1950; now the ratio is two to one. It took three West Germans to match the output of one American in 1950; now the ratio is less than three to two. U.S. productivity has not even kept pace with countries normally considered economically stagnant. For manufacturing industries, productivity climbed 2.2 percent in the United States between 1966 and 1976. That was lower than in Britain (3.1 percent) and Italy (5.3 percent). Other Western industrial economies far out-stripped the U.S. performance. West Germany posted a 5.8 percent gain. Japanese manufacturing climbed 8.9 percent in that period.

To some extent, productivity has climbed more rapidly in many Western countries because they had to make an all-out effort to catch up after World War II left their industries in ruins. That cannot explain all of the difference, however. Some believe

---

[29] The Federal Commission on Paperwork was established in 1976 by President Ford to study ways to eliminate bureaucratic barriers in the government's information network. See "America's Information Boom," *E.R.R.*, 1978 Vol. II, pp. 806-808.

[30] Quoted in *Congressional Quarterly Weekly Report*, June 16, 1979, p. 1155.

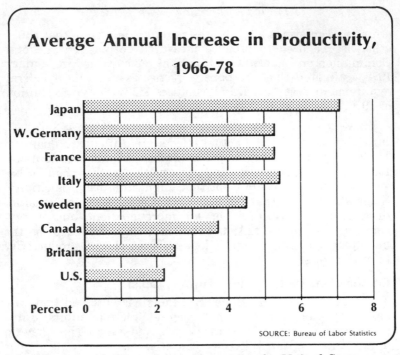

Average Annual Increase in Productivity, 1966-78

Japan

W. Germany

France

Italy

Sweden

Canada

Britain

U.S.

Percent   0   2   4   6   8

SOURCE: Bureau of Labor Statistics

that business, labor and government in the United States were slow to recognize the importance of maintaining productivity growth. Juanita Kreps echoed this view in leaving office Nov. 2 as Secretary of Commerce. She said the administration had put too much emphasis on things like weekly changes in the Consumer Price Index and not enough on tackling underlying problems such as the declining growth in productivity. Mrs. Kreps said she and other economic policy makers must share the blame for these shortcomings. "There've been times when I sensed that he [President Carter] was perplexed and may even be exasperated with the failure of the group to solve the problem [of the economy]."

Search for Solutions by U.S. and Business

If American economists were slow to recognize the productivity problem, they seem to be making up for lost time. Almost every week brings an announcement of a seminar, symposium, conference or lecture on the subject. Dozens of centers to study the problem have been established across the nation. "Every major university seems to have one," said Richard Landry, deputy economist for the U.S. Chamber of Commerce. "It's a growth industry."[31]

Many U.S. companies are setting up their own productivity programs, according to C. Jackson Grayson Jr., chairman of the

---

[31] Quoted in *The New York Times*, Oct. 29, 1979.

American Productivity Center in Houston. "What impresses me," Grayson said, "is the totality of the approaches. They are looking beyond industrial engineering to incentive schemes, employee involvement and new systems for management to gather information."[32] Some federal regulatory agencies are looking for ways to reduce the burden of government rules on business. Many of the proposed solutions to the productivity problem would encourage investment by increasing profits. The most-often heard proposals would: (1) reduce the corporate income tax rate, (2) liberalize the 10 percent tax credit on investments in new plant and equipment and certain business structures, and (3) allow businesses more rapid depreciation writeoffs.

Redesigning the Work Place

MANPOWER experts believe most efforts to improve productivity are doomed to failure if insufficient attention is given to worker attitudes. "With dollar-compensation no longer the overwhelmingly most important factor in job motivation, management must develop a better understanding of the more elusive, less tangible factors that add up to 'job satisfaction,'" William M. Batten said in his recent lecture at the Wharton School. "If we fail to develop the necessary philosophy and programs, we had better resign ourselves to coping with job tensions, attitudes and behavior that will limit productive output."

Many companies already are responding to the challenge. Some are making greater use of flexitime and other changes in work schedules to combat absenteeism and lessen worker discontent. The basic intention of a flexitime system is to allow workers greater flexibility in determining their starting and quitting times in a given work day. An employee who arrives at 7 a.m., for example, may leave at 3:30 p.m., and one who arrives at 9 a.m. may leave at 5:30 p.m. Usually there is a "core time" during which all workers must be present.

As many as two to three million Americans are working under some system of flexible hours, according to a recent survey.[33] Thousands of federal employees are participating in such programs in compliance with legislation passed by Congress in 1978. Most employees like flexitime, the survey reported, because they are better able to schedule their time in order to

---

[32] Quoted in *Time*, Aug. 27, 1979, p. 36.

[33] "Innovations In Working Patterns: Report of the U.S. Trade Union Seminar on Alternative Work Patterns in Europe," published jointly by the Communications Workers of America and the German Marshall Fund of the United States, May 1978.

minimize frictions between personal and family needs on the one hand and the requirements of the job on the other.[34]

Employers report that flexitime increases productivity by reducing absenteeism and virtually eliminating tardiness. Workers are less inclined to take a full or half day off when they wake up not feeling well, oversleep or have an appointment or problem to be attended. Workers tend to choose hours when they can be most effective on the job. Personnel turnover usually is reduced, lessening training and clerical costs and developing a higher quality work force. Workers tend to be willing to work longer hours, which would normally be considered overtime, during peak workload periods and take their compensatory time off during slack hours.

"Other advantages, intangible but no less real, also accrue to management," according to an article that appeared last year in *Business Horizons* magazine. "For example, flexitime naturally places on employees a greater sense of responsibility which, when transferred to the job itself, can induce better overall performance and closer identification with company objectives on the part of employees."[35]

Flexitime is not a panacea, however. Some supervisors say it makes it more difficult to schedule meetings and to communicate with employees. Furthermore, the system does not apply readily to all categories of workers. Airline pilots, hospital professionals and hundreds of other occupational groups involved in public services probably could not work flexible schedules. It is also a difficult system to implement for those on assembly lines whose jobs are closely integrated with the performance of co-workers.

Efforts to Improve the 'Quality of Work Life'

In addition to flexible working schedules, a growing number of companies are instituting "quality of work life" programs to give employees more control over day-to-day work patterns and, in some cases, a bigger voice in company policy. Such programs are operating in hundreds of companies, large and small, including "an important minority" of the *Fortune* "500," according to Richard E. Walton, professor of business administration at Harvard Business School.[36]

---

[34] The flexitime bill, signed by President Carter on Sept. 29, 1978, requires the Civil Service Commission to establish a voluntary program in selected executive agencies and military departments to test the effect of flexible hours on employees and their families, the efficiency of government operations, mass transit and energy consumption and federal government employment opportunities. See *1978 CQ Almanac*, p. 790.

[35] Robert J. Kuhne and Courtney O. Blair, "Flexitime," *Business Horizons*, April 1978, p. 42.

[36] Richard E. Walton, "Work Innovations in the United States," *Harvard Business Review*, July-August 1979, p. 91. The *Fortune* "500" are the nation's 500 largest industrial companies, as determined annually by the magazine.

Opting Out

For many Americans work is just another four-letter word. Fed up with the pressures — or the boredom — a growing number of people are opting out of the labor force to be supported by government, family or savings, Bernard Lefkowitz reports in his new book *Breaktime: Living Without Work in a Nine to Five World* (1979). "They probably would have stuck at it 20 years ago," he writes. "They would have carried their complaints home and vented them at the dinner table.... Then they would have answered the call of the morning alarm. The reason they don't now is that 'new sanctions' have been granted them to express their dissent in the most direct and personal manner.... They feel free to quit. They have received permission for 'the new routines' they want to develop."

Voluntary unemployment is not the only alternative to the nine-to-five grind. More instances are being reported of two persons sharing a job between them so that each can take on outside work, attend classes or enjoy leisure activities. The Bureau of Labor Statistics reports that about one-fifth of all jobs in the nation are held by part-time workers. And according to the bureau's reckoning, only about one part-timer in five actually wants to work full-time.

The Federal Employees Part-Time Career Act, which became law on Oct. 10, 1978, increased part-time job opportunities in the federal Civil Service. Permanent part-time work programs also have elicited support from lawmakers in California, Maryland, Massachusetts and Oregon.

Quality-of-work-life projects come in as many shapes and sizes as the companies which have created them. Some involve "work teams," eliminating the isolation of the worker who does one task repeatedly in favor of group projects in which responsibility for a variety of tasks is shared. Others give workers an opportunity to design their own assembly lines or work stations to make them more pleasant or efficient. In some plants autonomous production teams, operating without direct supervision, help select and train new team members, forecast material and manpower requirements and evaluate their own performances. Other companies have set up labor-management committees to help solve job problems.

Sidney Harmon, a former Commerce Department aide who ran a pioneering quality-of-work-life program at his own factory in Tennessee, stressed that such projects do not start with "piped-in music or employee swimming pools or other paternalistic benefits that 'we,' in our wisdom and generosity, provide 'you'; rather it is workers' sharing fully in making the decisons that design their lives at work." "Workers possess an enormous untapped inventory of know-how," Harmon continued. "If they ever believed they were genuinely respected for what they know, were truly part of the action, they would jolt our economists and pundits with what they would produce."[37]

There still is a lot of suspicion about quality-of-work-life programs — by both management and labor. Some managers are reluctant to give up any control over the work place. Unions, on the other hand, sometimes have trouble convincing members that such programs are not a management gimmick to increase productivity and weaken the union, or keep the union out. Daniel Zwerdling of the Association for Self-Management stressed the limits of such programs. "While workers gain some power and autonomy over their jobs," he wrote, "they must exercise them within a larger framework which has been dictated by corporate management. . . . The traditional power relationship . . . remains essentially unchanged."[38] Zwerdling said the same was true of some of the employee ownership plans now gaining popularity in the United States.

Employee Ownership: Democracy at Work

The most rapidly growing form of worker ownership in the United States is the Employee Stock Ownership Plan (ESOP). The Employee Stock Ownership Council in Los Angeles estimates there are about 3,000 ESOPs in the country. Although such plans vary, usually a fixed amount of stock is placed in a trust as collateral for a loan drawn on a bank. As the loan is paid off, the stock held in trust is conveyed to the employees, generally in proportion to their wages. Voting rights of stock held in trust usually are restricted and the proceeds usually serve as a deferred compensation plan.

In a recent *Harvard Business Review* article, James O'Toole said the principal motivation for establishing an employee stock ownership plan is economic, not democratic. "There are tremendous economic advantages, particularly to small- and medium-size companies, in the creation of ESOPs," he wrote. "Among the fabled benefits . . . are tax deductions for payments to principal as well as to interest on loans obtained through an employee trust and significant savings in estate taxes for an owner, who can pass on a company to his heirs without a public stock offering. Workers cooperate in such tax prestidigitation because they are promised significant increases in retirement incomes as a result of ESOP trusts."[39]

---

[37] Quoted in the *Chicago Tribune,* Sept. 17, 1979.

[38] Daniel Zwerdling, *Democracy at Work: A Guide to Workplace Ownership, Participation and Self-Management Experiments in the United States and Europe* (1978), p. 3. The Association for Self-Management, located in Washington, D.C., describes itself as "an open democratic association for the study of self-management, and the enhancement and development of self-management and organizational democracy." Besides holding occasional regional workshops and publishing a quarterly newsletter on self-management developments, the association has sponsored a series of international conferences on self-management.

[39] James O'Toole, "The Uneven Record of Employee Ownership," *Harvard Business Review,* November-December 1979, p. 188.

O'Toole analyzed the impact of employee ownership on employee morale, motivation and productivity. The effects were most positive, he concluded, when: (1) ownership is direct, that is, not through a typically designed ESOP trust; (2) ownership is widespread, that is almost all workers are shareholders, not just managers or those workers who are sophisticated enough to take the initiative to invest; and (3) ownership is broadly held, that is, when all workers have significant, not just minimal equity. "Title to a few shares in a large company does not fool anyone into thinking he or she owns it," O'Toole wrote. "People will only act like owners when their equity is sufficient. When people are actually owners of a company, they act with impressive productivity."[40]

On the basis of worker productivity and morale, cooperatives appear to be the most successful form of worker capitalism. Among the oldest and most successful cooperatives in the United States are 16 plywood manufacturing plants in the Pacific Northwest. According to Daniel Zwerdling, the mills operate under strictly egalitarian principles. Each worker owns one share of the factory and casts one vote in company-wide elections.

For the foreseeable future, worker-ownership is likely to be confined to a relatively small number of companies in the United States and continue to lag behind Western Europe, where worker participation is more advanced.[41] Many corporate executives remain skeptical of any worker participation schemes. "There are fears voiced by some managers," said Ted Mills, director of the American Center for the Quality of Work Life, "that encouraging increased 'participation' by the workforce means the opening of a Pandora's box, a first step toward encroachment upon management's prerogatives of controlling and directing the means and processes of production."[42] Despite these reservations, most business leaders now recognize the need to develop programs that address the problem of worker dissatisfaction and encourage workers to maximize their contributions to the productivity of the organizations that employ them.

---

[40] O'Toole's conclusions are supported by the findings of a study of 98 employee-owned companies conducted by the University of Michigan's Survey Research Center. See Michael Conte and Arnold S. Tannenbaum, "Employee-Owned Companies: Is the Difference Measurable?" *Monthly Labor Review,* July 1978, pp. 23-28.

[41] See, for instance, *Collective Bargaining and Worker Participation in Western Europe, North America and Japan,* The Trilaterial Commission, 1979.

[42] Quoted in Zwerdling, *op. cit.,* p. 179.

Selected Bibliography

Books

Denison, Edward F., *Accounting for Slower Economic Growth*, The Brookings Institution, 1979.

Lasch, Christopher, *The Culture of Narcissism*, W. W. Norton & Co., 1979.

Lefkowitz, Bernard, *Breaktime: Living Without Work in a Nine to Five World*, Hawthorn Books, 1979.

Levitan, Sar A. and William B. Johnston, *Work Is Here to Stay, Alas*, Olympus Publishing Co., 1973.

Sheppard, Harold L. and Neal Q. Herrick, *Where Have All the Robots Gone? Worker Dissatisfaction in the '70s*, The Free Press, 1972.

Terkel, Studs, *Working*, Pantheon Books, 1972.

Zwerdling, Daniel, *Democracy at Work*, Association for Self-Management, 1978.

Articles

"Big Crusade of the '80s: More Rights for Workers," *U.S. News & World Report*, March 26, 1979.

Bowen, William, "Better Prospects for Our Ailing Productivity," *Fortune*, Dec. 3, 1979.

Conte, Christopher R., "Productivity Lag Menaces U.S. Standard of Living," *Congressional Quarterly Weekly Report*, June 16, 1979.

Cooper, M. R., et al., "Changing Employee Values: Deepening Discontent?" *Harvard Business Review*, January-February 1979.

Kuhne, Robert J. and Courtney O. Blair, "Flexitime," *Business Horizons*, April 1978.

"New Breed of Workers," *U.S. News & World Report*, Sept. 3, 1979.

O'Toole, James J., "Dystopia: The Irresponsible Society," *Management Review*, October 1979.

——"The Uneven Record of Employee Ownership," *Harvard Business Review*, November-December 1979.

Sheehy, Gail, "Introducing the Postponing Generation," *Esquire*, October 1979.

Staines, Graham L. and Robert P. Quinn, "American Workers Evaluate the Quality of Their Jobs," *Monthly Labor Review*, January 1979.

Walton, Richard E., "Work Innovations in the United States," *Harvard Business Review*, July-August 1979.

Reports and Studies

"Contemporary Economic Problems," American Enterprise Institute, 1979.

Editorial Research Reports: "Productivity and the New Work Ethic," 1972 Vol. I, p. 291; "Four-Day Work Week," 1971 Vol. II, p. 607; "Blue-Collar America," 1970 Vol. II, p. 627; "Technology Gap: Reality or Illusion," 1978 Vol. II, p. 945.

"Innovations In Working Patterns," The Communications Workers of America and the German Marshall Fund of the United States, May 1978.

Meier, Gretl S., "Job Sharing," W. E. Upjohn Institute for Employment Research, February 1979.

Stokes, Bruce, "Worker Participation — Productivity and the Quality of Work Life," Worldwatch Institute, December 1978.

Two-Income Families

by

William V. Thomas

July 13
1 9 7 9

TWO-INCOME FAMILIES

W ITHOUT THEM, the good life would be out of reach for millions of American families. With their help, families that otherwise would be struggling to make ends meet are enjoying $100,000 homes, $12,000 cars and $5,000 European vacations. Expensive department stores and exclusive restaurants count on their business. They are part of the reason for the upsurge in private school enrollment and the boom in real estate investment.[1] Remove them from the picture and a sizable portion of the nation's buying power would disappear.

They are working wives, and today there are over 20 million of them in this country, according to the Bureau of Labor Statistics.[2] Two-income families constitute an increasingly powerful economic group. Working husbands and wives are generally young, well-educated, career-oriented and free-spending. There are 18.7 million working couples nationwide,[3] and nearly one-fourth of them are between the ages of 24 and 34. Families with two wage earners working full- or part-time had an annual median income of $21,064 in 1978, or $6,037 above that of single-earner households.

With 49 percent of all married women now working,[4] wives who stay home soon may become as unusual as women who worked in offices and factories once were. Last year, according to the Bureau of Labor Statistics, 58 perent of the women with school-age children were working; 41 percent of the mothers with children too young to attend school also had jobs.[5] Columbia University sociologist Eli Ginzberg has called the employment of women outside the home the most important social change of the 20th century. "But its long-term implications," he

---

[1] See "Private School Resurgence," *E.R.R.*, 1979 Vol. I, pp. 285-304, and "Housing Restoration and Displacement," *E.R.R.*, 1978 Vol. II, pp. 861-880.

[2] The Bureau of Labor Statistics reported in March 1979 that there were 22.8 million married women in the work force. This includes women who are working and women who are actively looking for work.

[3] The number of working wives exceeds the number of working couples because some husbands are unemployed or unable to work.

[4] The Bureau of Labor Statistics reported in March 1979 that 51 percent of all American women 16 and older held jobs or were looking for work.

[5] Bureau of Labor Statistics figures for March 1978.

Married Women in the Work Force

Year	All Women (add 000)	Married Women (add 000)	Percentage of Working Women Who are Married
1971	32,132	18,530	40.8%
1972	33,320	19,249	41.5
1973	34,561	19,821	42.2
1974	35,892	20,367	43.0
1975	37,087	21,111	44.4
1976	38,520	21,554	45.0
1977	39,374	22,377	46.6
1978	40,971	22,789	47.6

SOURCE: Bureau of Labor Statistics

added, "are absolutely unchartable. It will affect women, men and children, and the cumulative consequences of that will only be revealed in the 21st and 22nd centuries."[6]

The rapid increase in the number of working wives can be traced in part to the fading of the social stigma that used to be attached to married women — especially mothers — who held jobs. Today, a good job is as much a status symbol for a wife as it is for a husband. But an equally compelling factor encouraging wives to work is financial need. The rising cost of living has forced many married women to enter the job market, not simply to earn money for family necessities, but to afford the luxury items middle-class Americans have come to expect.

Keeping Up With the Cost of Inflation

Today's two-income couples can afford a life-style most single-income households cannot. Compared to older affluent couples, they tend to spend money more casually on travel, entertainment and recreation. In fact, spending money itself seems to have become a form of recreation for many young husbands and wives. But rising inflation, some confess, has made it difficult to ever really feel wealthy. "The costs so far outdistance the value," said one young Washington lawyer, "you don't feel at the top of the ladder at all."[7]

Consumer prices spiraled upward at an annual rate of 10.9 percent for the first five months of 1979. Housing, transportation, food and clothing all showed substantial increases. In addition, American budgets have been squeezed by rising Social Security payments and the higher federal income taxes that

---

[6] Eli Ginzberg, quoted by Caroline Bird in *The Two-Paycheck Family* (1979), p. xii-xiii.
[7] Quoted in James Fallows, "Washington: Fat City," *The Atlantic*, July 1979, p. 6.

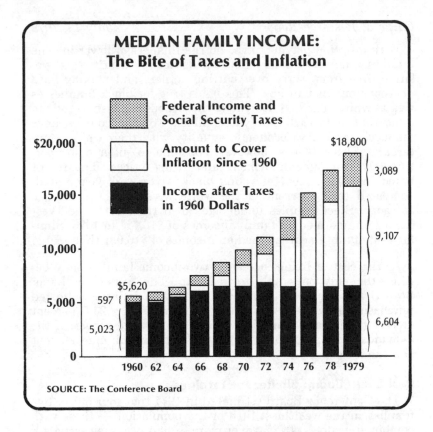

MEDIAN FAMILY INCOME:
The Bite of Taxes and Inflation

Federal Income and
Social Security Taxes

Amount to Cover
Inflation Since 1960

Income after Taxes
in 1960 Dollars

$20,000

$18,800

15,000

3,089

10,000

9,107

$5,620

5,000

597

6,604

5,023

0

1960 62 64 66 68 70 72 74 76 78 1979

SOURCE: The Conference Board

come with rising earnings.[8] The Conference Board, an independent economic research organization, reported in May that the
average family now must earn almost double its 1970 pretax
income to maintain the same standard of living it had nine years
ago. For example, a family of four earning $13,200 in 1970 now
requires over $25,000 to equal its 1970 purchasing power. This is
up from $23,000 last year.[9]

"The experts and people themselves have said it again and
again," Caroline Bird wrote in her new book, *The Two-Paycheck
Family*. "When the prices are high, it takes two to get ahead."[10]
Women have put themselves to work to defend a standard of
living they see threatened. "Most don't have the option of
working inside the home or outside the home anymore," said
Alexis M. Herman, director of the Women's Bureau of the Labor
Department. "Economic needs require that they go out and get
a job."[11]

[8] See "Social Security Reassessment," *E.R.R.*, 1979 Vol. I, pp. 461-480.
[9] The Conference Board, "The Two-Way Squeeze, 1979," Economic Road Maps No.
1852-53, April 1979.
[10] Bird, *op. cit.*, p. 8.
[11] Quoted in *The New York Times*, May 7, 1978.

With inflation playing havoc on the finances of lower-income families, many two-salary households occupy a privileged position, free from worry over cutting corners and making hard decisions on what to buy. This holds true for black families as well as white. The U.S. Bureau of the Census released a study in June that indicated that young black working couples have managed to achieve economic equality with their white counterparts. Other blacks, however, continue to suffer disproportionately from unemployment and rising prices. The report noted that 45 percent of young black wives work year round, compared to 33 percent of the white wives in the same age category. Black couples under age 35 in the North and West earned annual median family incomes of $16,715 in 1976. Similar white families earned median incomes of $16,691 that year.[12]

As the cost of living increases, two-income families may become the only ones able to keep up. The Bureau of Labor Statistics reported in July that the median inflation-adjusted purchasing power of two-income households was 23.5 percent greater than that of families with only one wage earner. If the demands of inflation draw more wives into the job market, that gap can be expected to widen.

Real Estate Boom: Shelter for Earnings

The Conference Board estimated in 1977 that four out of five families in the wealthiest fifth of the population — those with combined incomes of $25,000 or more — had two wage earners.[13] With taxes threatening a larger portion of their salaries *(see box, p. 65)*, one of the things these families are doing to protect their earnings is investing in real estate. The U.S. League of Savings Associations reported that 45 percent of all home buyers in 1977 were two-income families.

"Single-income families want the most modern homes, with everything showy," said David Costa, a real estate broker at Swanson Associates in Winchester, Mass. "The double-income couple likes older houses with character."[14] This new interest in older homes is responsible for the revitalization of many inner-city neighborhoods across the country. But it also has contributed to housing inflation at all levels. According to the National Association of Home Builders, the median cost of new homes rose from $23,400 in 1970 to $55,700 in 1978. During that same period, the cost of used homes went up from $23,000 to $48,700.

---

[12] U.S. Bureau of the Census, "The Social and Economic Status of the Black Population in the United States: An Historical View, 1790-1978," June 1979.

[13] Fabian Linden, "The Two- and Three-Income Family," *Across the Board*, May 1977, p. 49-51. *Across the Board* is a monthly publication of the Conference Board.

[14] Quoted in *Time*, Aug. 21, 1978, p. 56.

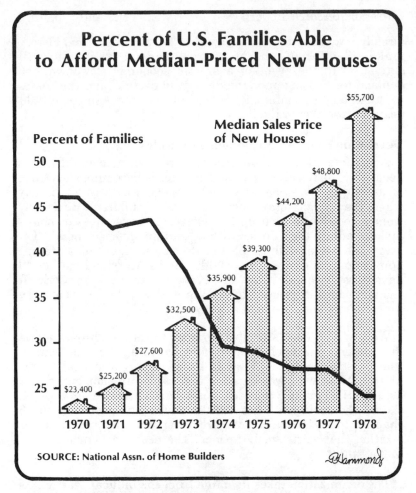

Percent of U.S. Families Able to Afford Median-Priced New Houses

Percent of Families

Median Sales Price of New Houses

$55,700

$48,800

$44,200

$39,300

$35,900

$32,500

$27,600

$25,200

$23,400

50

45

40

35

30

25

1970 1971 1972 1973 1974 1975 1976 1977 1978

SOURCE: National Assn. of Home Builders

Hammond

"Real estate isn't just [a tax] shelter anymore," said David Jensen, a real estate salesman in Farmington Hills, outside Detroit. Young couples with money to spend are "really buying for investment. They're betting on inflation. They keep buying . . . because the tax laws encourage it — the government is really paying for all of this — and they've figured out that there's no point in living in a $100,000 house if you can get a mortgage on one for $125,000. The more the house costs, the more money they're making as it keeps appreciating."[15]

As a result of the increasing cost of housing, mortgage debt has nearly doubled over the last five years. New and used homes still appear to be a good investment in most markets. But Alfred L. Malabre, news editor of *The Wall Street Journal,* warned that during an "infationary spiral a point ultimately will arrive when enjoyment turns to misery. . . . If the current inflation,

---

[15] Quoted in *Esquire,* July 3, 1979, p. 8.

already in double digits, is allowed to keep accelerating, history makes clear that jobs and the economy eventually will shrivel."[16] In the event of a drastic economic slowdown, the demand for housing undoubtedly would decline, and the homes couples bought at inflated prices hoping to make money would begin to lose their value.

Decreasing Emphasis on Homemaker Role

At a time when double incomes are seen as a middle-class necessity, the full-time wife and mother is becoming something of an oddity. Working wives often speak wistfully of the day when they might stay home and raise children. But many women today who identify themselves as housewives or home-makers admit they do so with a certain defensiveness. "For every one person telling me I'm doing the right thing staying home and taking care of my child," said a Maryland mother, "I have three people telling me I should go back to work. It shouldn't be a dirty word to say I'm a housewife. But that's the way you're sometimes made to feel."[17]

Women who decide to give up jobs to raise children believe they deserve as much support and encouragement as women who pursue careers. A Virginia-based organization called the Martha Movement was organized in 1976 with that purpose as its goal. The group's founder, suburban housewife Jinx Melia, claims the movement has 6,500 dues-paying members in 75 chapters in all 50 states. "We are a national membership organization that exists solely to meet the needs of homemakers," Melia said.[18]

The organization takes its name from the biblical Martha. As recounted in Luke's Gospel, Martha, the sister of Mary, invites Jesus into her home, and is then distracted by domestic chores while other guests listen to his philosophy. The parable, the Martha Movement suggests, is an apt metaphor for the current lack of importance attached to homemaking. "We feel that most of today's attention is to the Marys, with Martha continuing unrecognized," says one of the group's brochures.

The movement is avowedly non-ideological, a stance that has earned it the opprobrium of some other, more politically ori-ented women's groups. The Marthas have been criticized for not taking a stand on such issues as government-supported child care, the Equal Rights Amendment and abortion. In response,

---

[16] Alfred L. Malabre, writing in *The Wall Street Journal*, June 7, 1979.

[17] Quoted in *The Washington Post*, May 5, 1978.

[18] Quoted in *The New York Times*, Oct. 29, 1977.

members contend the Martha Movement was never meant to address political issues. Its chief function, Melia said, has been to set up a "network of support" through newsletters and meetings for women who have determined that the role of wife and mother is more important than that of a supplementary wage earner. In a society where buying things has become one of the last remaining activities that holds a family together, Melia said, the Marthas are searching for ways "to strengthen our marriages, raise our children and keep our wits."[19]

Wives in the U.S. Work Force

HISTORIANS have traced the "economic liberation" of married women back to the late 19th century when the growth of American industry put an end to the family as the chief economic unit of production. The affluence that accompanied industrialization swelled the ranks of the middle class, making it possible for many women to remain at home. But the expansion of business and industry also created new jobs for women, and thousands moved into positions in offices and factories previously held by men. Among the four million working girls and women counted in the 1890 census, about 500,000 were married.

Despite the growing employment of women, the popular turn-of-the-century notion was that wives should not take jobs. Homemaking was looked upon as a vocation in itself. That attitude waned, however, with America's entry into World War I, when women joined the work force in unprecedented numbers. Feminist leaders in the campaign for women's suffrage were convinced that a new era of equality was dawning. Margaret Drier Robbins told the Women's Trade Union League in 1917: "At last, after centuries of disabilities and discrimination, women are coming into the labor [market] on equal terms with men."[20]

But such optimism was premature. After the war, both employers and male employees tried to force many women to relinquish the new jobs and skills they had acquired. The male-dominated AFL unions led the fight for legislation to exclude women from certain blue-collar occupations. In some areas, women were barred from night work and overtime, effectively

[19] *Ibid.*
[20] Quoted by William Henry Chafe in *The American Working Woman: Her Changing Social and Political Roles, 1920-1970* (1972), p. 49.

eliminating them from high-paying jobs in fields like printing and transportation.

Despite these restrictions, more women were working than ever before. By the end of the 1920s, the female labor force had grown to 10.7 million from 8.4 million the previous decade, a 26 percent increase. Women were entering clerical and sales work in increasing numbers. Frederick Lewis Allen noted in *Only Yesterday* (1931), his account of the 1920s, that after passage of the suffrage amendment in 1919, middle-class girls "poured out of schools and colleges into all manner of occupations." But according to Professor William Henry Chafe of Duke University, historians have overstated the amount of economic change which occurred in the decade.

> There is no evidence that a revolution took place in women's economic role after World War I [Chafe wrote], nor can it be said that the 1920s represented a watershed in the history of women at work. . . . Aspiring career women were still limited to positions traditionally set aside for females; the overwhelming majority of American working women continued to toil at menial occupations for inadequate pay; and the drive to abolish economic discrimination enlisted little popular support.[21]

The number of married women entering the labor force grew steadily. By 1940, 17 percent of all women who worked were married. Still many people continued to oppose married women working, particularly during the Depression. A Gallup Poll in 1936 found that 82 percent of the population objected. In the late 1930s, bills were introduced in 26 state legislatures to keep married women from holding jobs. Only one of these passed. This was in Louisiana, and it was later repealed.

World War II and the New Consumer Age

World War II had profound effects on the U.S. economy and the status of working women. The war effort opened millions of new jobs to women, and female workers entered the labor force as never before. They accounted for 36 percent of the nation's jobholders in 1945, up from 25 percent in 1940. Wages rose, the number of working wives doubled and unionization of women quadrupled. In general, employers' attitudes toward women workers remained skeptical, but since women were the only available labor, they were hired.

The war gave women access to more skilled and higher-paying jobs. Previous bans on the employment of married women were discarded; by 1944, married women comprised almost half of the female labor force. Although the war made rapid changes in

---

[21] *Ibid.*, p. 51.

women's economic status, it did not make a lasting or profound difference in the public attitude toward working women, nor did it lead to greater equality between the sexes. Women continued to receive less pay than men, to be denied opportunities for advancement and to work in separate job categories. During the war, concluded William Henry Chafe, "traditional attitudes toward women's place remained largely unchanged."

After the war, women were expected to return to their traditional role of homemaker. Behind the efforts of employers, educators, social workers and the media to persuade women to leave the work force were two important economic considerations, said the editors of *America's Working Women:* "On the one hand, the system could not provide full employment; on the other hand, continued industrial profits required, with the diminution of military spending, an expansion in the consumption of household durable goods. An emphasis on 'homemaking' encouraged women to buy."[22]

This view overlooked the fact that the majority of women were working for economic reasons. A Department of Labor survey in 1945 found that 96 percent of all single women, 98 percent of widowed and divorced women and 57 percent of the married women seriously needed to continue working after the war. Many women were laid off in heavy industries. But for the most part, these women did not return to their kitchens. At the same time the war economy was changing into a consumer economy, significant changes also were occurring in the workplace. The rapid shift from manufacturing to service industries created new technical and office jobs in which brute strength was not a prerequisite and in which women could feel comfortable.

During the postwar baby boom,[23] when large families were the rule, many married women with children started back to work to help meet rising costs. Although the overall proportion of female workers fell to 28 percent after the war, thousands of housewives took full- or part-time jobs to supplement family incomes. Working wives of the 1940s and 1950s, according to Professor Chafe, "provided the indispensable condition for the middle-class life for millions."[24] They went to work, he added, not out of any great desire for self-fulfillment, but to increase their families' buying power in the new consumer age.

---

[22] Rosalyn Baxandall, Linda Gordon and Susan Reverby, eds., *America's Working Women* (1976), pp. 83-84.

[23] The baby boom spans the period from 1946 through 1964. In those 19 years, 76.4 million babies were born in the United States. Annual births rose from 2.9 million in 1945, before the boom began, to a peak of 4.3 million in 1957. From 1954 to 1964, there were more than four million babies born each year.

[24] Quoted in *The New York Times*, Nov. 30, 1978.

During the 1950s, the largest increase in labor force participation was among married women beyond the usual childbearing years (20 to 34). Working wives generally were regarded as "cakewinners" rather than "breadwinners," since their wages often provided extra money to buy luxury items families could not afford on the husband's salary alone. As a result, many married women were shunted into low-paying jobs with little chance for advancement. It was not uncommon for employers to pay them at a lower rate than single women or men doing the same work.

Outlawing Sex Discrimination on the Job

This practice and other forms of sex-related job discrimination have been banned by state and federal laws enacted over the last two decades. The first of these was the federal Equal Pay Act of 1963. It required all employers subject to the Fair Labor Standards Act[25] to provide equal pay for men and women performing similar work.

The following year, Congress passed the Civil Rights Act of 1964. Title VII of that act prohibited discrimination based on sex — as well as race, religion and national origin — in hiring or firing, wages, promotions or any terms or conditions of employment. Exceptions were permitted only when sex was a bona fide occupational qualification, as in the case of an actor or a model. Title VII is administered by the Equal Employment Opportunity Commission, whose five members are appointed by the president. Initially, the powers of the EEOC were limited largely to investigation and conciliation, but Congress amended the act in 1972 to let the agency go directly to court to enforce the law.

Because sex discrimination sometimes takes forms different from race discrimination, the EEOC issued sex-discrimination guidelines. They stated that the refusal to hire an individual cannot be based on assumed employment characteristics of women in general. The guidelines also prohibited hiring based on classification or labeling of "men's jobs" and "women's jobs," or advertising under male and female headings.

The EEOC guidelines declared that state laws that prohibited or limited the employment of women, such as those barring them from work immediately before or after childbirth, discriminate on the basis of sex because they do not take into account individual capacities and preferences. Forms of discrimination against married women, while not specifically

---

[25] The Fair Labor Standards Act of 1938 established a minimum wage for individuals engaged in interstate commerce or the production of goods for commerce. The law has been amended several times to increase the minimum rate and to extend coverage to new groups of employees.

forbidden, are considered by the commission to be in violation of its broader anti-sex bias rules.

In October 1967, President Johnson issued an executive order prohibiting sex discrimination and other forms of bias in hiring by federal contractors. The order required federal contractors to take "affirmative action" to ensure that applicants are employed and that they are treated during employment without regard to their race, color, religion, sex or national origin."[26] Other federal laws, orders and regulations have prohibited employment discrimination in special occupations or industries. For example, Title IX of the Education Amendments of 1972 specifically prohibited sex discrimination in education.

"After World War I. . . , the overwhelming majority of American working women continued to toil at menial occupations for inadequate pay, and the drive to abolish economic discrimination enlisted little popular support."

William Henry Chafe, *The American Working Woman: Her Changing Social and Political Roles* (1972)

The movement to end sex bias in employment and pay "is evidence of how interested women are in work, regardless of their motives in seeking it," *The Wall Street Journal* stated last year.[27] But figures cited in the *Journal* indicated that a majority of women working today hold clerical jobs and on the average earn about $6 for every $10 earned by men. That ratio has not changed greatly since 1955 when the government first began keeping such data.

Pregnancy Pay: Boost for Working Wives

In a sweeping expansion of the rights of working married women, the 95th Congress passed legislation in October 1978 to ban employment discrimination on the basis of pregnancy and require disability and health insurance plans to cover pregnant workers. The law amended Title VII of the 1964 Civil Rights Act to ban discrimination against all pregnant women in any area of employment, including hiring, promotion, seniority rights and job security. It also required employers who offered health insurance and temporary disability plans to extend coverage to women for pregnancy, childbirth and related medical conditions.

---

[26] See "Reverse Discrimination," *E.R.R.*, 1976 Vol. II, pp. 561-580.
[27] *The Wall Street Journal*, Oct. 28, 1978.

Consumer Price Index

(Annual Average Changes)*

1946	8.5%	1957	3.6%	1968	4.2%
1947	14.4	1958	2.7	1969	5.4
1948	7.7	1959	0.8	1970	5.9
1949	−1.0	1960	1.6	1971	4.3
1950	1.0	1961	1.0	1972	3.3
1951	7.9	1962	1.1	1973	6.2
1952	2.2	1963	1.2	1974	11.0
1953	0.8	1964	1.3	1975	9.1
1954	0.5	1965	1.7	1976	5.8
1955	−0.4	1966	2.9	1977	6.5
1956	1.5	1967	2.9	1978	7.6
				1979	10.9**

* For urban wage earners and clerical workers; U.S. city average, all items, not seasonally adjusted.

**Annual average through May.

Source: U.S. Bureau of Labor Statistics

The law was intended to reverse a 1976 Supreme Court decision, *General Electric v. Gilbert,* which held that employers need not include pregnancy in their disability pay plans. In 1976, writing for the court's 6-3 majority, Justice William H. Rehnquist said the exclusion was not discriminatory because "there is no risk from which men are protected and women are not. . . ." In dissent, Justice William J. Brennan Jr. wrote: "Surely it offends common sense to suggest . . . that a classification revolving around pregnancy is not, at the minimum, strongly 'sex-related.' "[28]

Supporters of pregnancy disability pay argued that discrimination based on pregnancy was at the root of women's employment problems because employers' views on pregnancy had relegated many women of childbearing age to marginal, low-wage positions. Opponents of the bill, including the U.S. Chamber of Commerce, countered that pregnancy is a voluntary condition that should not be regarded as an illness. They also expressed concern over the high cost of the legislation, citing estimates of $571 million a year for disability payments and $1 billion for health and medical expenses.

Opposition to one of the bill's provisions came from within the ranks of the women's movement. The legislation allows employers to exempt elective abortions from health insurance coverage. Representatives of a number of women's groups argued that the anti-abortion provision was unnecessary, since the legislation by its very nature was "pro-life" and "pro-family." The extension of disability benefits and job security to pregnant workers, they

---

[28] Also dissenting were Justices Thurgood Marshall and John Paul Stevens.

74

said, would encourage women to carry their babies to term rather than electing to have abortions. In addition, the payment of pregnancy benefits would prompt more women to go back to work after having children.

Impact on Society and Families

THE CHILDREN of the "permissive generation" of the late 1940s and 1950s have become the working husbands and wives of the present "acquisitive generation." The oldest postwar babies are now 33. Over the next ten years, their ranks will swell the typically big-spending 34-to-44 age group from its current 28 million to 40 million. According to Data Resources, a private economic organization, there are now 12.2 million couples in that age bracket. In a decade, there are expected to be 18.2 million.

Because of their growing numbers, the "baby boom" adults are being wooed by merchandisers of all kinds. Married couples are the most avidly courted, since they have more money to spend. As *Time* magazine described them, "baby boomers" were children of inflation, "born with credit cards in their mouths and oriented toward spending rather than saving. They are part of the instant-gratification, self-indulgent Me decade, which has a taste for high-priced gadgets and little interest in self-denial."[29]

Advertising seems to be keeping pace with this generation as it grows older, catering particularly to what is often regarded as its "almost religious" sense of self-esteem. These are the first adults to have been exposed to television all their lives. They are also the first generation to have grown up under the shadow of the Atomic Age. That combination, some social critics theorize, has created in many young adults a kind of "live now" mentality, encouraging them to buy what they want, when they want it — a craving that often requires two incomes to be satisfied.

New Division of Labor Within the Home

Nearly half (48 percent) of those responding to a 1977 *New York Times-CBS News* poll said they believed the most "satisfying" marriages were those in which both husband and wife worked and both shared the housework and child-rearing responsibilities. Some 43 percent favored the traditional marriage in which the husband was the breadwinner and the wife stayed home and took care of the house and children. The poll

[29] "The Over-the-Thrill Crowd," *Time,* May 28, 1979, p. 39.

also indicated a warming of public attitudes toward working mothers. More than half of those interviewed said that working mothers were better than, or as good as, their non-working counterparts. Only 40 percent said that working women would be worse mothers, compared to 48 percent who agreed in a similar poll conducted in 1970.[30]

"Men are beginning to recognize that they no longer need work all their lives at jobs they don't like to support wives and children. Women are beginning to question the ways in which women have adopted their careers to childbearing and some are questioning whether to have children at all."

Caroline Bird, *The Two-Paycheck Marriage* (1979)

Experts differ over the implications of these findings. Some see the growing acceptance of working wives and mothers as a positive step in the movement toward a more equitable society, while others see it as a threat to the stability of the family. Women who enter the marketplace develop "more self confidence . . . and gain a greater sense of economic worth," wrote Caroline Bird.[31] But they often have less time to spend on child care, homemaking and other functions that wives traditionally have performed. Psychologist Kenneth Keniston and other family experts have wondered if this change could have an unhealthy effect on "the content and nature of family life."[32]

Although most husbands welcome the additional income from their wives' jobs, many have a hard time adjusting to the new demands that go along with it. Being married to a woman with a busy schedule, an income of her own, and outside friendships and commitments may cause a husband to feel insecure and resentful. Numerous studies have shown that there is more divorce among families in which the wife works.[33] Once society has adjusted to women's new roles, the divorce rate might decline somewhat. But some observers believe that as the economic advances of women continue to alter their status in marriage, divorces are apt to increase.

---

[30] See *The New York Times*, Nov. 27, 1977.

[31] Bird, *op. cit.*, p. 11.

[32] Kenneth Keniston, *All Our Children: The Family Under Pressure* (1977), p. 5.

[33] See Heather L. Ross and Isabel V. Sawhill, *Time of Transition: The Growth of Families Headed by Women* (1975), pp. 35-66.

Closely related to this issue is the question of how the employment of women affects the division of labor within the home. In general, husbands of working wives engage in slightly more child care and housework than do husbands of non-working women. A 10-year study on housework by Professor John P. Robinson of Cleveland State University indicated that from 1965 to 1975 the amount of time working women devoted to doing household chores declined from 26 to 21 hours a week. The time men spent on housework during the same period increased from nine to 10 hours weekly. Robinson found that full-time homemakers in 1975 spent about 44 hours a week on housework, a drop from 50 hours in 1965.[34]

"The baby boomers . . . are a part of the instant-gratification, self-indulgent Me generation, which has a taste for high-priced gadgets and little interest in self-denial."

Time magazine, May 28, 1979

In many homes where both partners have jobs, the problem of dividing housework is often solved by hiring outside help. This has caused a shortage of domestic employees in some cities. It also has created a whole new service industry designed to meet the needs of working couples who do not have time to take care of routine domestic tasks, such as paying bills, handling deliveries and shopping. The owner of a San Francisco "errand" service called "Rent-a-Wife" described his business as an "idea whose time has come." "Someone has to be there for the phone company or the plumber," said a Los Angeles woman who runs a similar service. "People who work hard deserve to forget the little things," she said. "What's the sense of being successful if you can't enjoy it."[35]

Childless Couples; 'Commuter' Marriages

Many couples today are achievement-oriented.[36] They believe they are entitled to pursue their own interests — even if it

---

[34] See John P. Robinson, "Changes in Americans' Use of Time, 1965-1975," Cleveland State University, 1979.

[35] Both were quoted in the *Los Angeles Times,* Jan. 16, 1979.

[36] Two out of three parents interviewed in a 1976 survey conducted by Yankelovich, Skelly and White, a national market research and public opinion organization, said that parents should have their own lives and interests even if it means spending less time with their children. See "Raising Children in a Changing Society, The General Mills American Family Report, 1976-77."

means spending less time with their children, or not having children at all. The decision not to have children is often one that is not made consciously. Many times, it is the result of a tacit decision "not to decide," said Charles Westoff, head of the Princeton University Office of Population Research. Couples involved in their careers can gradually "back into childlessness," Westoff said.[37]

The U.S. birth rate in this decade is at its lowest point in history — the average family now has 1.8 children, about half the number of 20 years ago. Experts foresee a continued decline. A 1977 study on the falling birth rate by the Rand Corporation, a private research bureau, linked the drop to an increase in female employment. And as wages for women workers go up, the study predicted, the birth rate can be expected to decline even farther.[38]

"People are willing to take on any assignment, move to any location that promises a bigger paycheck — not for their family's well-being but for their own personal prestige."

William Raspberry, *The Washington Post*,
June 8, 1979

Among working couples who have children the trend is to rely on day-care centers and babysitters to supply the supervision they cannot. There also has been an increase in what sociologists call "latchkey children" — children unsupervised for portions of the day, usually between the end of the school day and the time when working parents return home.

Just as couples with careers tend to see less of their children, some, it seems, also see less of one another. Those with careers in separate cities sometimes practice what are being called "commuter" or "long distance" marriages, seeing each other on weekends or as time permits. The Census Bureau has no statistics to show how many couples actually maintain separate households. But, according to sociologist Betty F. Kirscher of Kent State University, such arrangements appear to be on the rise, especially in marriages where women hold "high-status" jobs that entail frequent transfers.

---

[37] Quoted in *The Washington Post*, April 9, 1979.
[38] See "The Emergence of Countercyclical U.S. Fertility," The Rand Corporation, 1977.

Company Couples

As an increasing number of women pursue professional careers, more and more companies find themselves in the position of having employees whose spouses work for clients, competitors or government regulators. As a result, many couples and companies face the delicate task of devising a new definition of conflict of interest. The situation has developed so rapidly, however, that few formal rules have been established.

"Conflict of interest between spouses is much more nebulous than something like owning stock in a supplier," said Lionel D. Norris of Atlantic Richfield. "We just have no specific policy." But the fact remains that many companies are afraid to hire people who might trade "business secrets" with their mates.

Despite the increase in working wives, many firms still have strict prohibitions against hiring married couples. A few companies have broken with that tradition, however. Citibank of New York, for example, lifted its ban against hiring husbands and wives in 1974. The federal Equal Employment Opportunity Commission has ruled that policies against hiring couples are legitimate if they are enforced without regard to sex. Nevertheless, couples that do work for the same company frequently are prohibited from working in the same department or having authority to promote each other. "The husband and wife may bend over backward to be professional," said Pamela Turner, director of placement for the Sloan School of Management at M.I.T., "but the situation makes other people feel awkward."

For both men and women, economic security has become a matter of paramount importance. Most people, wrote *Washington Post* columnist William Raspberry, "are willing to take on any assignment, move to any location that promises a bigger paycheck — not for their family's well-being but for their own personal prestige."[39] Too often, Raspberry concluded, the outcome is not more happiness, but less. In their quest "to stay ahead," many two-income couples have eliminated the problems caused by not having enough money. But in their haste, they could be setting the stage for future regrets — the kind that may surface when they begin to wonder if the pursuit of money was worth the price.

[39] Writing in *The Washington Post,* June 8, 1979.

Selected Bibliography

Books

Bird, Caroline, *Born Female: The High Cost of Keeping Women Down,* Pocket Books, 1971.
———— *Enterprising Women,* New American Library, 1976.
———— *The Two-Paycheck Family,* Rawson, Wade Publishers, 1979.
Chafe, William Henry, *The American Woman: Her Changing Social, Economic and Political Roles, 1920-1970,* Oxford University Press, 1972.
Jongeward, Dorothy and Dru Scott, *Affirmative Action for Women,* Addison-Wesley, 1975.
Kreps, Juanita, *Sex in the Marketplace: American Women at Work,* The Johns Hopkins Press, 1971.
Quinn, Jane Bryant, *Everyone's Money Book,* Delacorte, 1979.

Articles

"America's New Elite," *Time,* Aug. 21, 1978.
Bettleheim, Bruno, "Untying the Family," *The Center Magazine,* September-October 1976.
" 'Company Couples' Flourish," *Business Week,* Aug. 2, 1978.
Harris, Marlys, "Couples Wedded to the Same Careers," *Money,* Jan. 28, 1978.
Hayghe, Howard, "Families and the Rise of Working Wives — An Overview," *Monthly Labor Review,* May 1976.
Kron, Joan, "The Dual Career Dilemma," *New York,* Oct. 25, 1976.
Nulty, Leslie E., "How Inflation Hits the Majority," *Challenge,* January-February 1979.
Smith, Robert, ed., "The Equal Employment Opportunity Commission and How to Make it Work," *Ms.,* February 1977.
"The Over-the-Thrill Crowd," *Time,* Aug. 21, 1979.
Ware, Ciji, "Is a Baby Worth the Price?" *New West,* April 25, 1977.

Reports and Studies

Butz, William P. and Michael P. Ward, "The Emergence of Countercyclical U.S. Fertility," The Rand Corporation, 1977.
Editorial Research Reports, "Child Care," 1972 Vol. II, p. 439; "Single-Parent Families," 1976 Vol. II, p. 661; "Women in the Work Force," 1977 Vol. I, p. 121; "The Changing American Family," 1977 Vol. I, p. 412.
Espenshade, Thomas J., "The Value and Cost of Children," *Population Bulletin,* April 1977.
Nulty, Leslie E., "Understanding the New Inflation: The Importance of the Basic Necessities," Exploratory Project for Economic Alternatives, 1977.
The Conference Board, "The Two-Way Squeeze, 1979," April 1979.
U.S. Bureau of the Census, "The Social and Economic Status of the Black Population in the United States: An Historical View, 1790-1978," June 1979.
U.S. Department of Labor, "Why Women Work," 1976.
————, "1975 Handbook on Women Workers," 1975.

VIETNAM WAR

LEGACY

by

Marc Leepson

**July 6
1 9 7 9**

VIETNAM WAR LEGACY

WHEN the last American troops withdrew from Vietnam on March 29, 1973,[1] there was no victory celebration. The troop withdrawal signaled the end of nearly a decade of American participation in the Vietnam War — a conflict that took 55,000 American lives and brought about unprecedented divisiveness at home between those who supported the war and those who protested against it. The fact that this country failed to meet its objective in Vietnam — that we did not win the war — added to the nation's uneasy feelings. It is little wonder that after the war was over, the last thing most Americans wanted to discuss was Vietnam.

But the war will not go away. Within the last two years, books, films, television shows and plays have examined the war and its impact on American society. The war's bitterest memories have faded and the reassessments have not engendered national turmoil. What is taking place is a sober examination of why we got involved in Vietnam and what the war's consequences have been for the United States. "The Deer Hunter," a controversial movie about three American soldiers in Vietnam, sparked much of the new interest when it came out last year. From the advance notices, it would appear that another wave of national interest could surface when Francis Ford Coppola's long-awaited Vietnam War movie "Apocalypse Now" opens in this country in mid-August.

Recent Novels and Non-Fiction Accounts

Vietnam veterans and former war correspondents have led the way in setting down their thoughts about the war in novels and memoirs, the best of which have been published only within the last three years. One example is Marine veteran Ron Kovic's bittersweet memoir, *Born on the Fourth of July,* which came out in 1976. Kovic wrote about growing up on Long Island in the 1950s, joining the Marines out of a sense of patriotism after graduation from high school, and volunteering for Vietnam. Kovic's world was shattered near the end of his second tour of duty when a .30 caliber machinegun bullet tore into his lung and

---

[1] The last Americans — including 800 Marine guards — were evacuated from Vietnam when Saigon fell to the communists on April 30, 1975.

severed his spinal column. Today he is paralyzed from the chest down.

The principal contribution of *Born on the Fourth of July* is its powerful portrayal of a paralyzed veteran whose life becomes a tortured nightmare. "It has been a long odyssey for me, a long journey through darkness," Kovic told an interviewer when the book was published. "When I finished the book, I began to come out of eight years of incredible depression, nightmares, sickness, suicidal tendencies. . . . It's like a phoenix from the ashes — just a tremendous physical, mental, emotional and political resurrection."[2]

The two best fictional accounts of the war — Tim O'Brien's *Going After Cacciato* and James Webb's *Fields of Fire* — were published last year. O'Brien's surreal story, his third book dealing with Vietnam, tells of an infantryman named Cacciato who decides to escape the fighting in Vietnam by walking to Paris. The book won the prestigious National Book Award for fiction this year. Critic Pearl K. Bell wrote: ". . .O'Brien sheds more light on the state of mind induced by the incomprehensible peculiarities of Vietnam than anything else I have so far read about that wasted and unavailing conflict."[3]

Webb, like O'Brien a Vietnam combat veteran, uses the conventional war-novel format in *Fields of Fire*. He tells the story of a group of soldiers from different backgrounds trying to stay alive in Vietnam. But *Fields of Fire* rises above the war novel cliches. It is a frighteningly believable story about the horrors of war and the madness of the military. Other novels dealing with Vietnam include Robert Stone's *Dog Soldiers* (1974) and Larry Heinemann's *Close Quarters* (1977).

---

[2] Quoted in *The Washington Post,* Aug. 10, 1976.

[3] Pearl K. Bell, "Writing About Vietnam," *Commentary,* October 1978, p. 77.

Of the non-fiction works, three stand out: *Dispatches* (1977) by *Esquire* magazine's Vietnam correspondent Michael Herr; *A Rumor of War* (1977) by journalist and former Marine lieutenant Philip Caputo; and *Friendly Fire* (1976) by novelist C. D. B. Bryan. Reviewers have praised all three for capturing the essence of the Vietnam War and its effects on those who served, their families and friends. Bryan said of *Dispatches* when it was published: "Nothing else so far has even come close to conveying how different this war was from any we fought — or how utterly different were the methods and the men who fought for us."[4] Bryan's *Friendly Fire* describes an Iowa farm family's anguished reaction to their son's accidental death in Vietnam. The book was made into a three-hour television movie this year. *Washington Post* television critic Tom Shales called the show, which was seen by some 60 million Americans April 22, "the most straightforward and heartbreaking dramatic work done on the Vietnam War and made available to a mass audience."[5]

Hollywood's Portrayal of America at War

One way to illustrate the vast differences between the Vietnam War and other 20th century American wars is by examining the movies made about each. The American motion picture industry, then in its infancy, strongly supported the American effort in World War I. Stars like Charlie Chaplin and Mary Pickford appeared at Liberty Bond rallies at movie theaters nationwide. Films such as "Red Cross Nurse" (1918), starring Marie Dressler, extolled the American fighting man and portrayed Germans as "beastly Huns" in an effort to boost morale on the home front. Even Hollywood's top director, D. W. Griffith, made three stridently anti-German movies. "Seldom, if ever, had so much venom been channeled through the medium of the screen," authors Richard Griffith and Arthur Mayer wrote of that filmmaking era.[6] The anti-German tone subsided after the war. Griffith, for example, made a 1924 film, "Isn't Life Wonderful," that sympathetically portrayed the plight of a German family.

Hollywood repeated the patriotic effort during World War II. That war "...was, for Hollywood, a remake of World War I," film critic Richard Corliss wrote, "but with sound and music and an all-star cast. Straight-faced, lantern-jawed, with a little stubble, Our Hero machoed his way over the beaches of Omaha and Guam and into the hearts of gorgeous Resistance leaders."[7]

---

[4] Writing in *The New York Times Book Review*, Nov. 20, 1977.

[5] *The Washington Post*, April 19, 1979.

[6] Richard Griffith and Arthur Mayer, *The Movies* (1957), p. 115.

[7] Richard Corliss, "Guns & Buttered Popcorn: Hollywood Reels in the War," *New Times*, March 20, 1978, p. 66.

In 1942 alone, 80 pictures were released dealing with war themes, according to Griffith and Mayer. Shortly after the war, several movies examined the plight of the veteran. "The Best Years of Our Lives," the story of three returning veterans, won the Oscar for best film of 1946. By the late fifties, several movies, including "The Young Lions" (1958), showed compassion for the Germans and questioned some aspects of how the United States fought the war.

Unlike World Wars I and II, the Korean War spawned only a handful of patriotic combat movies. Most of them portrayed American soldiers as gritty combat heroes — even though they did not win the war. Two Hollywood movies of the late 1950s may be interpreted as pacifist allegories. Neither "Paths of Glory" (1957), set in World War I, nor "Bridge On the River Kwai" (1959), set in World War II, carried a patriotic pro-war message, as did the World War I and II war movies.

The Vietnam War was slow to capture Hollywood's attention. "For once, America went to war without the movie industry," Richard Corliss wrote. Until 1977, only one major motion picture about the war was released: "The Green Berets" (1968), starring John Wayne. *New York Times* film critic Vincent Canby described Wayne's only directorial effort as "ludicrously gung-ho."[8] Two years ago, a spate of films about the war, including "Heroes," "Rolling Thunder" and "The Boys in Company C," were released. They attempted to portray the unique experiences of those who served in Vietnam.

"There were over 500 movies made about World War II," Joseph Maxwell (Max) Cleland, the head of the Veterans Administration, told Editorial Research Reports. "All of them conveyed a basic, silent message — that the American soldier was the good guy. I think the movies about Vietnam ... bespeak the complex nature of that war — no more clear-cut good guys and bad guys. There are shades of complexity and shades of difference."

Max Cleland

The two most prominent Vietnam War movies — "Coming Home" and "The Deer Hunter" — were released to critical and popular acclaim in 1978. "Coming Home's" message was solidly anti-war. Jon Voight played the hero, a paraplegic Vietnam veteran who falls in love with Jane Fonda,

---

[8] *The New York Times*, Feb. 19, 1978.

the wife of a pro-war Marine officer. Fonda, one of the leading anti-war activists, won the Oscar for best actress of 1978. Voight, who also supported the anti-war movement, won the Oscar for best actor.

The Academy Award to Voight brought more than honor to him. It also helped the image of the Vietnam veteran. "When you have millions of people looking at an event together and all of a sudden the best actor is the guy who played the disabled Vietnam veteran in a gripping movie, in effect the image of the Vietnam veteran has kind of taken a dramatic turn," said Max Cleland, himself a disabled Vietnam veteran. "Because what was the image of the Vietnam veteran before? Drug addicted, walking time bomb, psychopathic killer, a guy who was a misfit and couldn't make it. That was the image of Vietnam veterans in movies."

While there was some criticism of the movie's artistic merits, most observers commented favorably about "Coming Home's" portrayal of Vietnam veterans. "Historically speaking, 'Coming Home' is an honest attempt to come to terms with one agonizing aspect of the war," wrote Peter Arnett, who won a Pulitzer Prize in 1966 for his coverage of the war for the Associated Press. "The movie is one of the most achingly accurate representations of the Vietnam experience yet made. . . ."[9]

'The Deer Hunter' and 'Apocalypse Now'

Michael Cimino's "The Deer Hunter," won three Academy Awards, including best picture of 1978. The movie showed what happened to three friends from a steel-mill town in western Pennsylvania after volunteering to fight in Vietnam. One is killed, one badly wounded and the other returns home even more mentally disturbed than before he left. Jane Fonda, film critic Pauline Kael and author Gloria Emerson,[10] among others, have complained that the movie unfairly depicts the Viet Cong as blood-thirsty killers and the Americans as innocents in a corrupt land.

John Pilger of the London *Daily Mirror* wrote that "The Deer Hunter" appealed "directly to those racist instincts that cause wars and that allowed the Vietnam War to endure for so long — a movie that reincarnated the triumphant Batman-jawed Caucasian warrior, that presented the Vietnamese as Oriental brutes and dolts, and that served up a new form of gratuitous violence in the orgiastic Russian-roulette scenes that never, to my knowledge, happened, and with John Wayne-like heroes and

---

[9] Writing in *The Miami Herald*, April 15, 1979.

[10] Emerson's book *Winners and Losers* (1977) described the impact of the Vietnam War on the lives of a number of Americans. Emerson covered the war for *The New York Times* from 1970-72.

heavenly violins thrown in."[11] Director Cimino insists the movie does not take a pro-war stance and that the Russian roulette scenes were merely a cinematic metaphor to show the horror of war.

Initial reaction from American critics who have seen Francis Ford Coppola's soon-to-be released "Apocalypse Now" has been very favorable. Susan Heller Anderson of *The New York Times* wrote that "each minute is so packed with detail that the collective impact leaves the spectator stunned."[12] The film, which *Variety* on May 16 called "the most widely heralded production of the last 10 years," was named co-winner of the best picture award at this year's Cannes Film Festival in France. Inspired by Joseph Conrad's *Heart of Darkness*, "Apocalypse Now" stars Marlon Brando as an Army colonel who "goes native" in the Vietnamese jungle. The Brando character experiences horrors akin to the dark visions that haunted Conrad's Mr. Kurtz in the Congo. Industry sources say the film will be the most expensive movie ever produced and will need to earn at least $50 million to break even.

In addition to the award-winning books and movies, four plays opened this year in New York City dealing with the Vietnam War: Elizabeth Swados' rock musical based on Michael Herr's *Dispatches;* David Berry's "G. R. Point," starring Michael Moriarty; and James McLure's one-act comedies "Lone Star" and "Pvt. Wars." Those productions were preceded by playwright David Rabe's trilogy dealing with the military during Vietnam, "The Basic Training of Pavlo Hummel," "Sticks and Bones" and "Streamers."

Problems of War's Veterans

SOME 2.6 million men served in Vietnam from Aug. 4, 1964, when President Johnson asked Congress to approve the Gulf of Tonkin Resolution, to May 7, 1975, when President Ford issued an executive order officially ending all American involvement in the war.[13] Unlike those who served in America's other wars, the Vietnam veterans received no heroes' welcomes when they returned home. On the contrary, many Americans viewed those who fought in Vietnam with fear and suspicion. Many Vietnam veterans came home to other problems as well: drug

---

[11] Writing in *The New York Times*, April 26, 1979.

[12] *The New York Times*, May 21, 1979.

[13] See "Vietnam Veterans: Continuing Readjustment," 1977 Vol. II, pp. 785-804.

Stamp Honoring Vietnam Vets

At the White House reception for Vietnam Veterans May 30, President Carter unveiled the design of a new U.S. postage stamp paying tribute to veterans of the Vietnam War. The stamp will be issued in Washington Nov. 11 in connection with the observance of Veterans Day. The  stamp's design features an enlarged replica of the Vietnam Service Medal that was awarded to those who served in Vietnam.

addiction; alcoholism; unemployment, especially among young black veterans; severe psychological readjustment problems, primarily among the 1.6 million combat veterans; and neglect and sometimes incompetent treatment from government agencies whose job it is to help them. One result: until recently many Vietnam veterans closeted themselves with their war experiences and, unlike veterans of other wars, did not immediately join together in self-help organizations.

"This country has tried to bury Vietnam in its subconscious, like a bad memory. We did not want to admit we were not successful at war," VA Administrator Cleland said May 16.[14] "We did not want to face the unprecedented discord it created in our society. We did not want to even talk about it. In trying to bury a painful war, we tend to forget those who gave the sacred sacrifice of life; we have dismissed the bravery of those who fought; we have ignored the contribution of all who served. As a result, too many Vietnam veterans were sorry they served their country, when they should have been proud."

New interest in the Vietnam War by the publishing and movie industries, the news media and the U.S. Congress has given Americans a new awareness of the special problems of the Vietnam veterans. "We've put enough time between us so that we can start to look at the problems of Vietnam veterans,"

---

[14] In a speech before the American Red Cross National Convention in Kansas City, Mo.

combat veteran Tim Kolly, a legislative assistant to Rep. David E. Bonior, D-Mich., told Editorial Research Reports. "We now have political leaders, we have people in journalism — in other words, people that are in positions to influence what goes on in government and what goes on in the minds of American people — who are sympathetic, who can now separate the war from the warrior and realize that the war was not the Vietnam veteran's fault." Vietnam veterans were officially honored last Veterans Day when President Carter dedicated a plaque in Arlington National Cemetery. A presidentially proclaimed Vietnam Veterans Week *(see below)* was observed for the first time during the last week in May.

Vietnam Veterans Congressional Caucus

Rep. Bonior, who served in the Air Force from 1968 to 1972, last year formed a congressional caucus — called Vietnam Veterans in Congress — to deal specifically with Vietnam veterans' problems. The group consists of Senators and Representatives from both parties with both liberal and conservative outlooks *(see box, p. 91)*. "I didn't come to Congress with any idea of getting involved in this issue," Bonior said in a recent interview. "When I came to Washington [in 1977], I assumed that like veterans of other wars . . . Vietnam veterans were being taken care of in reasonably good fashion. I guess I assumed wrongly."[15]

Bonior said he discovered that the veterans committees in Congress were dominated by veterans of World War II and Korea. "There weren't any Vietnam veterans on those committees," he said. Furthermore, except for Max Cleland, there were no Vietnam veterans in top policy positions in the Carter administration dealing with Vietnam veterans' problems. In addition, Bonior said, the traditional veterans lobbying organizations "weren't pushing Vietnam veterans programs. They had no people in leadership positions that were Vietnam veterans."

The veterans caucus lobbied successfully last year for a bill giving a tax credit to employers who hire Vietnam veterans. Bonior's group also sponsored a resolution establishing the last week in May as Vietnam Veterans Week. President Carter stressed the importance of paying "full tribute at last to all Americans who served in our armed forces in Southeast Asia," in his official message proclaiming Vietnam Veterans Week. "Their courage and sacrifices in that tragic conflict were made doubly difficult by the nation's lack of agreement as to what constituted the highest duty. Instead of glory, they were too often met with our embarrassment or ignored when they returned."

---

[15] Interview with Editorial Research Reports, May 31, 1979.

Vietnam Veterans Caucus

Rep. Les Aspin, D-Wis.	Rep. Albert Gore Jr., D-Tenn.
Rep. Don Bailey, D-Pa.	
Rep. Michael D. Barnes, D-Md.	Rep. Tom Harkin, D-Iowa
Rep. Douglas K. Bereuter, R-Neb.	Sen. H. John Heinz III, R-Pa.
Rep. David E. Bonior, D-Mich.	Rep. James R. Jones, D-Okla.
Rep. John J. Cavanaugh, D-Neb.	Rep. John J. LaFale, D-N.Y.
Rep. Thomas A. Daschle, D-S.D.	Rep. John P. Murtha, D-Pa.
Rep. Christopher J. Dodd, D-Conn.	Rep. Leon E. Panetta, D-Calif.
Rep. Allen E. Ertel, D-Pa.	Sen. Larry Pressler, R-S.D.
Rep. Martin Frost, D-Texas	Rep. Toby Roth, R-Wis.

Many Americans have seen Vietnam veterans as an "embarrassing reminder" of the war, Carter told an audience of some 400 persons, mostly Vietnam veterans, at a White House reception May 30. "Most of those who have returned have almost miraculously been able to assimilate back into civilian life," the president said in an emotional speech. But the fact that most veterans are doing well, he added, "is no comfort to those who've not been able to overcome physical or psychic problems of war. The nation has not done enough to respect, to honor, to recognize and reward the special heroism" of Vietnam veterans. The president pledged that the federal government will "change its attitude of neglect" toward Vietnam veterans. "The nation is ready . . . to recognize finally . . . the wisdom and experience and insight into the consciousness of America which you represent, and to honor your valor, sacrifice and commitment," Carter said.

New Psychological Adjustment Program

A House-Senate conference committee agreed during Vietnam Veterans Week on a new psychological counseling program for Vietnam veterans — another measure the veterans caucus had lobbied for. It had been 10 years since Max Cleland told a congressional committee that returning Vietnam veterans required special counseling to cope with emotional scars of the war and the rejection they encountered when they came home. Cleland argued then and now that Vietnam veterans need a special readjustment counseling program because psychiatric wards of VA hospitals are often understaffed or staffed with foreign doctors and because many troubled veterans distrust the VA or fear the stigma of being a psychiatric patient.

Four times since 1971, the Senate had approved a special counseling program. But skeptical old-line veterans' groups and their supporters in the House were cool to the idea, particularly since those pushing the program wanted much of it to be conducted outside the VA. But strong support this year from President Carter, Max Cleland and the veterans caucus, finally forced Congress to act.

Cleland, for one, is happy with the program. "It's going to have a minimum of paperwork," he said June 5. "We are going to set up a community-based operation that's going to talk to the guys and help them deal with their problems. That's what our goal is and by the end of the year I think we'll be well along in our nationwide effort on that." Some, including Rep. Bonior, have criticized the fact that the program has been allocated only $12.2 million out of a total VA budget of $20.4 billion. The veterans caucus had asked for $50 million. "We are pleased that the bill was passed," Bonior told Editorial Research Reports, "but we were disappointed in the fact that the money wasn't really substantial."

Recent studies have indicated a high incidence of combat-related psychological problems among Vietnam combat veterans. Although most Vietnam veterans have adjusted well to life back home, as many as 500,000 are experiencing varying degrees of emotional problems directly related to their war experiences. Psychologists began diagnosing what they term "post-Vietnam syndrome" in the early 1970s. Philip Caputo called the malady *"combat veteranitis,"* which he described as "an inability to concentrate, a childlike fear of darkness, a tendency to tire easily, chronic nightmares, an intolerance to loud noises — especially doors slamming and cars backfiring — and alternating moods of depression and rage that [come] for no apparent reason."[16]

Psychologist John Wilson of Cleveland State University in Ohio conducted in-depth interviews with some 400 Vietnam veterans from 1974 to 1977. Wilson reported that 25 percent to 33 percent of all Vietnam veterans and 40 to 50 percent of those who were closest to the fighting are struggling today with intense psychological problems, including alcoholism and drug addiction. Wilson estimated that as many as 500,000 Vietnam veterans are "suffering from a form of survivor reaction known as the delayed-stress syndrome."[17] This is characterized by "alienation, depression, guilt, anger, rage, shame, and feelings of rejection."

Charles Figley, a social psychologist and head of the interdisciplinary Consortium on Veterans Studies at Purdue University, conducted a similar study with 906 veterans in the East St.

---

[16] Philip Caputo, *A Rumor of War* (1977), p. 4.
[17] Writing in *The New York Times,* May 28, 1979.

Louis, Ill., area. He came up with about the same results as Wilson's research. Figley told Editorial Research Reports June 8 that the current attention being given to the Vietnam veterans is "a good, healthy sign, not only for the Vietnam veteran, but for the nation. Even though a lot of problems remain, for the vast majority of veterans of the Vietnam War, the last six months have been a godsend, primarily because they now know that they are being appreciated."

"The Vietnam veteran should be and can be viewed as a survivor of a disastrous event," Figley added, with symptoms such as loss of sleep, anxiety, difficulty with personal relationships and overuse of drugs to anesthetize memories. "How do we care for other survivors?" he continued. "We treat them with respect, concern, with love and caring. We treat the Vietnam veteran quite differently." Figley said that new public awareness of the Vietnam veterans' problems and the new VA counseling program will help many Vietnam vets with their psychological problems.

Formation of Veterans' Self-Help Groups

A nationwide group specifically for Vietnam veterans, Vietnam Veterans of America, was set up this spring with headquarters in Washington and New York City. Its organizer, Robert Muller, is a former Marine combat officer who is now a paraplegic. Muller had held a management position with the Paralyzed Veterans of America, one of the traditional veterans organizations. He left that organization early in 1978 to head the Council of Vietnam Veterans, which has given way to Vietnam Veterans of America.

Muller has worked closely with the congressional veterans caucus to lobby for jobs, education, health care and counseling for Vietnam veterans. "The first thing we're asking the administration to do," Muller said recently, "is to stop misrepresenting the situation to the public, and to stop putting out the line of rhetoric about how fine and dandy everything is for the Vietnam veteran. It isn't."[18] Another group working for Vietnam veterans is the Vietnam Veterans Foundation, headed by Vietnam veteran Tom Wincek. That group has concentrated on helping veterans own and operate small businesses and is pushing for benefits for Vietnam veterans operating small businesses similar to those given by the government to minorities.

Veterans' job prospects within the federal and state governments were given a boost June 5 when the U.S. Supreme Court upheld a Massachusetts law that gives veterans who pass a qualifying test the right to be hired before non-veterans. Oppo-

---

[18] Quoted in *The New York Times*, May 2, 1979.

nents argued that the veterans preference programs — which the federal government has had since 1944 — allow veterans to obtain government jobs at the expense of those who are not veterans, especially women. That situation, they say, is at variance with equal opportunity laws.[19]

The Disabled American Veterans (DAV), which sponsored Wilson's research at Cleveland State University, late last year organized its own nationwide outreach program to help Vietnam veterans. Six pilot "store-front" program centers were set up in Cleveland, Detroit, Atlanta, Baltimore, Denver and Los Angeles primarily to help Vietnam veterans with psychological problems. Initial reaction was so strong that the DAV decided to open centers in 67 other cities. The centers are staffed for the most part with Vietnam veterans. "The key to this whole program is the idea of one Vietnam veteran talking to another about problems that both can understand through their similar experiences," DAV National Director of Services Norman B. Hartnett said recently. "Hopefully, at each of these outreach locations, community agencies will provide on the spot many of the services that these veterans need — things like legal assistance, family counseling, and help with psychological problems."[20]

Effects of the Herbicide Agent Orange

At President Carter's reception for Vietnam veterans May 30, he was interrupted twice by unexpected questions from the audience. One questioner asked about government programs for veterans with pychological problems. The other questioner, veteran Frank McCarthy, shouted: "What about Agent Orange victims, President Carter? Thousands of our men are dying." McCarthy, president of Agent Orange Victims International, asked the president to implement a government study on the issue.

Some 12 million gallons of the defoliant Agent Orange were used to destroy millions of acres of Vietnamese jungle beginning in 1963.[21] After South Vietnamese newspapers began running stories claiming that Agent Orange caused birth defects and other medical problems, the U.S. Air Force stopped the aerial spraying in 1970. One of Agent Orange's ingredients is a substance called dioxin, one of the most toxic chemicals ever synthesized. Dioxin is so powerful that scientists measure its presence in parts per trillion. Within the last few years, thousands of

---

[19] See "Affirmative Action Under Attack," *E.R.R.*, 1979 Vol. I, p. 241.

[20] Quoted in *DAV Magazine*, November 1978, p. 9.

[21] See "Toxic Substance Control," *E.R.R.*, 1978 Vol. II, p. 756.

Vietnam veterans have contacted Veterans Administration hospitals complaining of a variety of illnesses they claim resulted from exposure to Agent Orange.

The VA on June 5 announced a broadening of its inquiry into possible effects of Agent Orange. Administrator Cleland said that a formal VA Advisory Committee comprised of 15 physicians and scientists and at least one Vietnam veteran would monitor all research and claims involving Agent Orange. The official VA position is that thus far no conclusive evidence exists linking Agent Orange to long-term health problems. Nonetheless, Cleland has said that he is "vitally concerned" about Agent Orange claims and has given "the highest priority" to the VA effort to find out if the chemical is responsible for illness among those exposed to it in Vietnam.

The VA was criticized for the way it has handled the Agent Orange question at a House subcommittee hearing June 26. Rep. Bob Eckhardt, D-Texas, chairman of the House Commerce Committee's Subcommittee on Oversight and Investigation, said the VA's failure to conduct research on veterans exposed to Agent Orange is a "national disgrace." The subcommittee heard testimony from Vietnam veterans Michael Ryan and John Woods, who claimed their children suffered birth defects due to Agent Orange. Ryan's 8-year-old daughter, who was born with 18 birth defects including brain damage and a partial spine, accompanied her mother and father to the hearing.

The Air Force recently began a study of some 1,200 servicemen who were directly exposed to Agent Orange in Vietnam. The study will compare that group with a large control group not exposed to the herbicide. The study is expected to take about six years to complete. The National Veterans Law Center, a public interest group, sued the VA May 31 on behalf of eight veterans suffering from disorders including brain cancer, liver dysfunction, nervousness, kidney failure and blackouts. The suit is an attempt to gain benefits for 330 veterans who filed claims with the VA. Attorney Lewis Milford of the center estimated that some 100,000 Vietnam veterans may have physical disabilities caused by Agent Orange.

Reassessment of War's Impact

JUST as the Vietnam War continues to play a role in the lives of many of its veterans, the war's memory is also alive among many Americans who did not serve in the armed forces.

Of the nearly 27 million men eligible for the draft during the Vietnam era, about 16 million did not serve in the military. To avoid the draft, many young men changed their lives drastically. Some married or had children sooner than they otherwise would have. Others pursued careers or academic studies they did not feel comfortable with. "The 26,800,000 men of the Vietnam generation are preoccupied with building careers, raising families, and making their way in American life," authors Lawrence M. Baskir and William Strauss wrote last year. "But their experience with the war can never be erased. Few can forget the decisions, compromises and sacrifices they had to make. The war may fade in everyone elses's mind but not in theirs."[22]

Some 96 percent of the men who did not serve in the military received deferments or were exempted or disqualified from military service, according to data compiled by Baskir and Strauss, members of the clemency board set up by President Ford in 1974 to review amnesty requests of draft evaders and deserters. Baskir and Strauss divided those who did not serve into four groups: (1) "avoiders," those who managed to avoid the draft by getting status deferments, physical exemptions or "safe enlistments" in the reserves or the national guard; (2) "evaders," who for the most part refused induction;[23] (3) "deserters," military men who illegally dropped out of the service; and (4) "exiles," the 50,000 men who fled either to foreign countries or underground in the United States. Of those who went to Canada, Sweden, Mexico and other countries, some 15,000 came home without penalty; 5,000 returned to the United States and went to prison; 17,000 were convicted and discharged from the military without going to prison; and 8,000 took advantage of President Ford's 1974 clemency program. The rest remain in exile.

On his first day in office, Jan. 21, 1977, President Carter fulfilled a campaign promise and issued a proclamation giving "a full, complete and unconditional pardon" to all those who committed any violation of selective service laws during the Vietnam era. Carter excluded only those who committed offenses involving violence. President Ford's amnesty proclamation of Sept. 16, 1974, offered amnesty to draft evaders and military deserters only after they pledged to complete up to two years of "alternative service." Only 6 percent of the roughly 350,000 eligible persons ever applied to the program, according to Baskir and Strauss. Of the 21,000 who applied, just 8,000 received the formal clemency offered by the program.[24]

---

[22] Lawrence M. Baskir and William Strauss, *Chance and Circumstance* (1978), p. 247.

[23] This group included about 200,000 accused draft offenders, some 4,000 of whom served prison sentences.

[24] Baskir and Strauss, *op. cit.*, p. 215.

The return of Marine Pfc. Robert Garwood to the United States March 25, 1979, raised new interest in the fate of those Americans listed as Missing in Action (MIA) in Southeast Asia. Garwood, who was captured by the Viet Cong in Da Nang in 1965, allegedly was brought out of a prisoner of war camp in 1969 to influence other American prisoners to cooperate with their captors. Garwood faces charges of deserting in time of war, unlawfully communicating with the enemy, urging American soldiers to refuse to fight and attempting to subvert the loyalty of other American prisoners.

The latest figures from the Pentagon's Office of Manpower Management Information list 129 American MIAs. These men are considered still alive and on active duty. At least 1,100 men whose remains have never been found are listed as "presumed dead." Are there other Americans living in Vietnam? A Vietnamese refugee said last year that he had seen more than 40 American prisoners of war in different parts of Vietnam as recently as April 1977. That claim came at the annual meeting of the National League of Families of American Prisoners and Missing in Southeast Asia in San Diego July 16, 1978. Ngo Phi Hung, who had escaped from Vietnam by boat to Thailand and arrived with his family in this country last June, told the group that he had seen the prisoners near the cities of Saigon, Tay Nhin, Ban Me Thuot, Nha Trang and Quang Ngai between June 1975 and April 1977. He said he obtained a list of the prisoners' names, but the list was stolen in Thailand and he could not remember any of the names. Hung repeated the assertions August 9, 1978, before the Asian and Pacific Affairs Subcommittee of the House Foreign Affairs Committee.

After the allegations were made public, the U.S. Defense Intelligence Agency (DIA) investigated the claims. The DIA issued an 86-page report in December which concluded that Hung was mistaken. "Based on the inconsistencies noted in Mr. Hung's story, DIA is not able to accept all his information as reliable and is unable to attribute credence to his report of live sightings," the report said.[25] The government of the Socialist Republic of Vietnam publicly announced on Aug. 11, 1978, in an official letter to the U.S. Department of State, that there was no truth to Hung's allegations.

Changing Views of American Involvement

Many Americans continue to view the Vietnam War as a total military failure for the United States. Dozens of books have been written chronicling how Presidents Truman and Eisenhower provided millions of U.S. dollars and military equip-

---

[25] U.S. Defense Intelligence Agency, "DIA Findings on the Report of U.S. POWS in Vietnam From Refugee Ngo Phi Hung," December 1978, p. 47.

The Boat People

"If the United States were to fail in Vietnam," President Nixon said in 1971, "if the communists were to take over, the bloodbath that would follow would be a blot on this nation's history from which we would find it very difficult to return." The U.S. withdrawal from Vietnam has produced no bloodbath thus far, but hundreds of thousands of Indochinese — Vietnamese, Cambodians and Laotians — either have escaped or have been forced out of their homelands. The statistics are staggering:

- 700,000 people have left Indochina since 1975, including some 250,000 Laotians and Cambodians and 200,000 ethnic Chinese from Vietnam
- 245,000 Vietnamese have escaped their homeland in boats
- 57,000 Vietnamese have settled in already overcrowded Hong Kong

It has not been easy for the refugees. Many — the "boat people" — are living in crowded boats in international waters waiting for a country to accept them. Malaysia, which since 1975 has given temporary asylum to some 118,000 Vietnamese, has expelled about 55,000 refugees this year. In June, the Malaysian government herded about 13,000 Vietnamese onto 60 vessels and sent them into international waters. Neighboring Indonesia's navy is keeping a 24-hour guard on its shores to keep the boat people out.

ment first to the French and then to the South Vietnamese, how President Kennedy ordered in the first American ground troops, how President Johnson escalated the war, and how President Nixon's "Peace with Honor" crumbled within two years after the last American troops left Vietnam.

Two new books question whether Vietnam was a total disaster for the United States. Guenter Lewy, who teaches political science at the University of Massachusetts, contends in *America in Vietnam* (1978) that the war was neither illegal nor immoral. "While the charges of American political and military ineptitude in Vietnam can be sustained by all the available evidence," Lewy wrote before the book was published, "and while the question of the overall prudence of justice of the American involvement is not easily resolved, the charges of officially condoned crimes and grossly immoral conduct are without substance."[26]

Leslie Gelb, who directed the official Defense Department history of the war — the "Pentagon Papers" — has written a new book, *The Irony of Vietnam: The System Worked,* which concludes that the American commitment to help South Viet-

---

[26] Writing in *Commentary*, October 1978, p. 29.

nam lasted from 1945 when President Truman began supplying military equipment to the French, to 1975. At that point, Gelb writes, "the domestic balance of opinion shifted and Congress decided to reduce support to Saigon in 1974-75 — that is, . . .the consensus, and hence the purpose, changed and the United States decided to let Vietnam go."[27]

New York Daily News reporter Harrison Rainie, who is writing a book about the press and Vietnam, agrees with Gelb. Rainie contends that the American public was not deceived by government secrecy and misleading statements about America's military role in Vietnam. Rainie concluded that "we knew what we were doing when the war was escalated and were well appraised of the consequences. In short, we had no logical reason to cry foul several years later and claim that all the facts had been withheld by malevolent leaders."[28]

Not all the new non-fiction accounts of American participation in Vietnam present the revisionist viewpoint. British journalist William Shawcross' new book, *Sideshow: Kissinger, Nixon and the Destruction of Cambodia,* is an outright condemnation of the way President Nixon and his Secretary of State, Henry Kissinger, ran the war in Vietnam and the invasion of neighboring Cambodia in 1970. Harvard University professor Stanley Hoffmann wrote that the book ". . .lays bare the fallacies and the shame of the Vietnam war with so much evidence and force that recent attempts at rewriting this tragic story in order to vindicate American policy appear as ludicrous as the policy itself."[29]

It will be decades before history's final judgment about America's participation in the Vietnam War is rendered. And it is a certainty that much more discussion of the war, its veterans and its effects on American society will be forthcoming in books, movies and in the media. "I think that we will stay fascinated with this question for quite a while," Max Cleland told Editorial Research Reports. "The need is going to be so great to talk, to deal with the issues because it is a part not only of the lives of Vietnam veterans, but it's a part of our national life too. And, in effect, we as a nation are emotionally amputated if we can't talk about it." Whether the new interest in Vietnam is an attempt to assuage national guilt or merely a propensity to re-examine the past, unarguably it is a constructive response to one of the nation's most destructive experiences.

[27] Leslie H. Gelb, with Richard K. Betts, *The Irony of Vietnam* (1979), p. 24.

[28] Writing in *Harper's*, July 1978, p. 23.

[29] Writing in *The New York Review of Books*, June 28, 1979, p. 3.

Selected Bibliography

Books

Baskir, Lawrence M., and William Strauss, *Chance and Circumstance: The Draft, The War and the Vietnam Generation,* Knopf, 1978.

Caputo, Philip, *A Rumor of War,* Holt, Rinehart, 1977.

Emerson, Gloria, *Winners and Losers,* Random House, 1977.

Figley, Charles R., ed., *Strangers at Home: Social Psychological Perspectives of the Vietnam Veteran,* Praeger, 1979.

——, *Stress Disorders Among Vietnam Veterans,* Brunner-Mazel, 1978.

Gelb, Leslie H., with Richard K. Betts, *The Irony of Vietnam: The System Worked,* Brookings Institution, 1979.

Herr, Michael, *Dispatches,* Knopf, 1977.

Kovic, Ron, *Born on the Fourth of July,* McGraw-Hill, 1976.

Lake, Anthony, ed., *The Vietnam Legacy: The War, American Society and the Future of American Foreign Policy,* New York University Press, 1976.

Thompson, W. Scott and Donaldson D. Frizzell, eds., *The Lessons of Vietnam,* Crane, Russak, 1977.

Articles

Bell, Pearl K., "Writing About Vietnam," *Commentary,* October 1978.

Corliss, Richard, "Guns & Buttered Popcorn: Hollywood Reels in the War," *New Times,* March 20, 1978.

Kidder, Tracy, "Soldiers of Misfortune," *Atlantic,* May 1978.

Kroger, William, "Whatever Happened to the Vietnam Veteran?" *Nation's Business,* December 1978.

Lewy, Guenter, "Vietnam: New Light on the Question of American Guilt," *Commentary,* October 1978.

Morrow, Lance, "Vietnam Comes Home," *Time,* April 23, 1979.

Schaar, Karen, "Vietnam Vets Still Fighting for Mental Health," *APA Monitor,* April 1979.

Stack, Dave, "Vietnam — the Unwelcome Veterans," *AFL-CIO American Federationist,* May 1979.

"The Vietnam War and American Values," *The Center Magazine,* July-August 1978.

Wehr, Elizabeth, "Psychological Aid for Vietnam Vets Approved," *Congressional Quarterly Weekly Report,* May 26, 1979.

Weinraub, Bernard, "Now, Vietnam Vets Demand Their Rights," *The New York Times Magazine,* May 27, 1979.

Reports and Studies

Editorial Research Reports, "Vietnam Veterans: Continuing Readjustment," 1977 Vol. II, p. 787; "Vietnam Veterans," 1973 Vol. I, p. 125.

Project Return-VETS, "Missing in America: The Hidden Minority of Vietnam Veterans," September 1978.

U.S. Defense Intelligence Agency, "DIA Findings on the Report of U.S. POWs in Vietnam From Refugee Ngo Phi Hung," December 1978.

AMERICA'S CHANGING SUBURBS

by

William V. Thomas

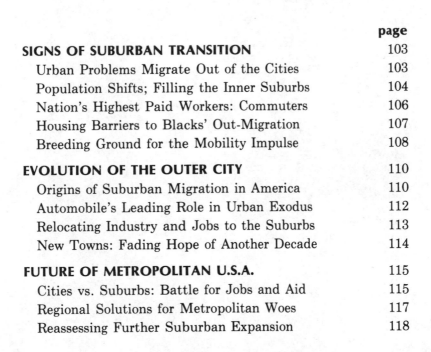

AMERICA'S CHANGING SUBURBS

P EOPLE went on a rampage. They threw rocks, smashed windows and fought with the police. There was, by all accounts, a complete breakdown of social order. A decade ago, it might have been identified as an expression of big city frustration. This particular uprising, however, began as a protest against high gasoline prices. That it took place in June in Levittown, Pa., once a synonym for suburban tranquility, suggests a troubling new sort of discontent may be brewing in the nation.

Long seen as a place to escape to, suburbia has been invaded by the outside world. Suburbanites, in one sense at least, are having to pay the price for the comfortable distance they've been keeping — higher fuel costs to indulge their long-distance lifestyle. But the suburbs are feeling the strain in other ways as well. If commuting is more expensive, so is the American Dream of climbing "the ladder of consumption." Inflation has driven up the price of everything from new homes to private school tuition. And all the while, the problems of the city — crime, overcrowding and neglect — are edging closer. Residents of the suburbs, wrote columnist George Will, "feel they are suffocating in the open air. . . . Suburbia's symbol, the cul-de-sac, expresses [their] mood on the eve of the 1980s. A cul-de-sac is, after all, just a fancy dead end."[1]

The gap between the reality and the myth of suburbia often makes it difficult to come to grips with the changes occurring there. Suburban life commonly evokes a romantic image of small, out-of-the-way residential villages, commuter train platforms and fleets of station wagons traveling back and forth from nearby city centers. The reality is usually very different. In recent years many suburban communities have become heterogeneous, urbanized areas where all of the traditional activities of the cities — and many of the city's troubles — can be found.

"This evolution has radically altered the exclusive residential character of older suburbs and former rural areas," wrote urban specialist James W. Hughes. "Yet with vigorous persistence, many suburban municipalities view themselves in the tra-

---

[1] George Will, writing in *Newsweek*, July 9, 1979, p. 84.

ditional mode, [with] little function beyond that of protecting a way of life they regard as unique."[2]

But it is precisely the uniqueness of suburban life, many believe, that is now being threatened. The suburbs are struggling with cities over a broad range of issues: integration, declining employment opportunities, transportation and housing for the poor. The barriers that once separated the suburbs from the city are gradually falling away.

A growing number of cities and neighboring suburban localities are pooling their resources and forming systems of regional government. In many sections of the country, judges are mandating an end to exclusionary zoning practices that have worked to keep low-cost housing and minorities out of the suburbs. And in what some see as the ultimate sign of change, 60 U.S. representatives from suburban districts joined together in 1977 to form the Congressional Suburban Caucus. Their goal — to plead for federal aid to help the suburbs provide needed jobs and services.

The energy shortage, increased population density and the added fiscal burdens brought on by more residents all have begun to shape new attitudes in suburbia. The "pull up the gangplank" mentality, while it has not entirely disappeared, has been tempered as suburbanites are beginning to admit social and economic realities that in years past might have easily been ignored.

Population Shifts; Filling the Inner Suburbs

In 1978, according to Census Bureau estimates, two-thirds of the U.S. population lived in the nation's 281 metropolitan areas,[3] with about three-fifths of that segment residing outside the central city in the surrounding suburbs. The fast suburban growth of recent decades slowed in the 1970s. And the central cities, with few exceptions, continued to lose population, especially the white population whose exodus had long been under way. While this population trend remains unchanged, it is also true, however, that many suburban whites have moved into the cities in recent years. During 1975-1977, the Census Bureau reported, 4.7 million whites moved from the cities to the suburbs. But slightly more than half that number, 2.5 million, left the suburbs and moved to the cities.[4]

---

[2] James W. Hughes, "Dilemmas of Suburbanization and Growth Controls," *The Annals of the American Academy of Political and Social Science,* November 1975, p. 65. Hughes is a professor of urban policy at Rutgers University.

[3] The Commerce Department defines a metropolitan area — formally designated a Standard Statistical Metropolitan Area — as any city, together with the county or counties where the city is located, which has a population of 50,000 or more.

[4] See "Social and Economic Characteristics of Metropolitan and Non-metropolitan Population: 1977 and 1970," Bureau of the Census, Special Studies P-23 No. 75.

Population Changes in Metropolitan America

During the first half of this decade the central cities lost population while the suburbs continued to gain. But the gain was less than in the 1960s, as shown in the following Census Bureau figures:

	1978 Population Estimates (millions)	Change From 1970 Census	1970 Change From 1960
U.S. total	213.5*	6.8%	13.3%
Metropolitan	143.0	4.4	16.6
Inside central cities	59.7	−5.0	6.5
Outside central cities	83.3	12.3	26.7
Non-metropolitan	70.4	12.2	6.8

While the black population of the central cities continued to rise and the white population declined, the percentage increase of blacks in the suburbs was nearly seven times greater than in the central cities, as shown below in official 1978 population estimates and percentage changes (in parentheses) since 1970:

	Whites (millions)	Blacks (millions)
Metropolitan	121.6 (2.3%)	18.4 (13.0%)
Inside central cities	44.5 (− 9.0)	13.7 (6.0)
Outside central cities	77.1 (10.2)	14.8 (39.1)
Non-metropolitan	63.2 (12.1)	6.3 (10.2)

* Excluding persons in the armed forces and in institutions. The total U.S. population as of Jan. 1, 1979, was estimated at 219.5 million.

Source: Bureau of the Census, "Population Profile of the United States: 1978," Series P-20, No. 336, issued April 1979.

Unlike the fluctuating racial makeup of central cities, the overall racial composition of the suburbs has been relatively constant. The labor force distribution by place of residence remained roughly the same as that of the population as a whole — about 30 percent in cities, 30 percent in rural areas, and 40 percent in the suburbs. Blacks constituted about 20 percent of the labor force in the cities and 5 percent in the suburbs.

From 1970 to 1977, the suburban population increased by 28 percent. That growth is likely to continue. But the suburbs face a problem of absorbing newcomers. Whereas cities tend to grow vertically, suburbia expands laterally. There is only so much space available for new growth, and some suburban communities have sought to slow development by restricting water and sewer hookups.[5] Many suburban areas have already reached their limits.

[5] See "Restrictions on Urban Growth," *E.R.R.*, 1973 Vol. I, pp. 87-104.

The first areas to feel the effect of blocked expansion are the inner suburbs. Contributing to the growing population of these sections are the masses of racial minority residents being priced out of their in-town homes to make way for restoration and renewal.[6] By Census Bureau estimates, of the 50 congressional districts that have lost 5 percent or more of their populations since 1970, 46 are predominantly urban, and almost all of these are largely filled with the non-white poor. Fourteen of 15 congressional districts represented by blacks have lost population since the last census, and New York's 21st congressional district, the country's only predominantly Puerto Rican district, lost nearly one-third of its people in less than eight years.

Between 1970 and 1976, 14 of the nation's 20 most populous cities lost residents to the suburbs *(see table, p. 111).* Much of the out-migration from cities ends in the near suburbs. The result is often overcrowding, decay and the eventual abandonment of neighborhoods by business and industry seeking more fertile fields for investment in the newer outlying suburbs.

Nation's Highest Paid Workers: Commuters

According to most economic indicators, suburban residents are better off financially than their counterparts in urban and rural areas. Unemployment rates for the suburbs are lower, and suburbanites generally enjoy higher earnings. "This does not mean that suburban residence is the key to better jobs and higher incomes," wrote Labor Department economist Diane N. Westcott. But it does suggest that residential location is an important factor contributing "to racial and economic inequities in jobs."[7] Of course, living in the suburbs is itself often the result of families having better jobs and making more money.

Research has shown that suburban workers are most likely to hold jobs outside of the communities where they live, and commuters usually earn higher incomes than those who live and work in the same vicinity. In 1975, about one-third of all U.S. workers, and nearly half (45 percent) of the suburbanites, traveled to jobs outside of their residential areas. Among persons living and working in central cities that year, only 13 percent had incomes above $15,000, whereas a significantly higher proportion earning $15,000 or more were commuters — 16 percent of those commuting from cities to jobs in the suburbs and 24 percent of those traveling from the suburbs to work in the city. Nearly half of the black workers holding jobs in the suburbs live in the cities.

---

[6] See "Housing Restoration and Displacement," *E.R.R.,* 1978 Vol. II, pp. 861-880.

[7] Diane N. Westcott, "Employment and Commuting Patterns: a Residential Analysis," *Monthly Labor Review,* July 1979, p. 8.

Congressional Districts With Non-White Majorities

District No.	City	Representative	Population Loss 1970-1976
Calif. 29	Los Angeles	Augustus F. Hawkins*	6%
Ill. 1	Chicago	Bennett M. Stewart*	15
Ill. 7	Chicago	Cardiss Collins*	12
Md. 7	Baltimore	Parren Mitchell*	9
Mich. 1	Detroit	John Conyers Jr.*	11
Mich. 13	Detroit	Charles Diggs*	19
N.J. 10	Newark	Peter W. Rodino Jr.	9
N.Y. 12	Brooklyn	Shirley Chisholm*	15
N.Y. 14	Brooklyn	Fred Richmond	11
N.Y. 19	Manhattan	Charles B. Rangel*	14
N.Y. 21	Bronx	Robert Garcia	29
Ohio 21	Cleveland	Louis Stokes*	21
Pa. 2	Philadelphia	William H. Gray III*	7
Tenn. 8	Memphis	Harold E. Ford*	9
Texas 18	Houston	Mickey Leland*	6

*Members of the Congressional Black Caucus. Other districts represented by blacks are: Ronald V. Dellums, D-Calif. (8th); Julian C. Dixon, D-Calif. (28th), Walter Fauntroy, D-District of Columbia, a non-voting delegate. Only Dellums' district did not show a population loss.

All representatives listed above are Democrats.

Of the people who lived and worked in the same community, suburbanites again had the highest average earnings, while rural residents had the lowest.[8] Not only do suburban residents tend to earn more than others, they also experience less unemployment. The Bureau of Labor Statistics reported that joblessness among suburbanites was 5.2 percent in 1978, well below that of central cities (7.4 percent) or rural areas (5.8 percent). Among suburban blacks, the rate was 10.5 percent, compared to 13.9 percent for urban blacks.[9]

Housing Barriers to Black Out-Migration

The sameness of many suburban communities is often the result of people with similar social and economic interests congregating in the same residential areas. In the compartmentalized environment of the suburbs, sharply defined groupings almost invariably follow along racial lines as well. "There is a deeply embedded and pervasive racial segregation within the social geography of suburbia," wrote Professor Peter O. Muller of Temple University.[10] Whereas blacks make up 11 percent of

---

[8] Statistics above are from "The Journey to Work Supplement," *The Department of Housing and Urban Development Annual Housing Survey*, 1975.

[9] Among white males 16 and older, the highest labor force participation rate (81 percent) was in the suburbs. But suburban black males were not far behind (77 percent). Suburban black women joined the labor force at the rate of 61 percent, substantially higher than that of their counterparts in other areas. White suburban women had a participation rate of 51 percent. The labor force includes all those either working or actively looking for work.

[10] Peter O. Muller, *The Outer City: Geographical Consequences of the Urbanization of the Suburbs* (1976), p. 18.

the U.S. population and 12 percent of the metropolitan population, they account for only about 6 percent of the nation's suburbanites. Lately, there has been a slight increase in the movement of blacks into the suburbs of many metropolitan areas, but not enough, observers say, to denote a significant shift in trends.

With rare exception, suburban America remains the exclusive preserve of whites. During the 1960s, according to the Census Bureau, more than 800,000 blacks moved into the suburbs. However, their numbers were dwarfed by the 15.5 million whites who moved there during the same period. From 1970 to 1978, the black suburban population grew by two-fifths, reaching 4.8 million. But whites continue to make up 94 percent of America's suburban residents. For blacks who do migrate to suburban neighborhoods, it has often meant exchanging one undesirable address for another.

Like their urban counterparts, blacks in the suburbs are frequently shunted into a separate housing market. They tend to be steered away from many white enclaves by real estate agents; and many banks, through loan discrimination, financially support the racial exclusivity of certain established neighborhoods. Despite ongoing efforts to modify this situation, little change has taken place. Sociologist J. H. Denton has written:

> . . .[B]y preventing the minority person from being able to shop for housing in the way that is normal for his white peers, a permanent barrier to residential desegregation has been created which may be beyond the power of positive law to reach.[11]

Fewer blacks live in the suburbs than appears warranted by the group's rising income levels. The consensus among researchers is that the cause of residential discrimination is not class difference but a persistent pattern of private and public discrimination. As a result, most middle-class blacks often seek housing in the best peripheral communities available and in this way manage to maintain a social distance from lower-class nonwhite minorities in central city neighborhoods.

Breeding Ground for U.S. Mobility Impulse

The deterioration of large cities, urban sprawl, suburban integration and a whole nexus of problems referred to as the "urban crisis" are associated with the mobility of people. While transcience itself has long been studied by demographers, popular concern over the propensity of Americans to move is rel-

---

[11] Quoted by Donald Foley in "Institutional and Contextual Factors Affecting the Housing Choice of Minority Residents," in *The Manipulated City: Perspectives on Spatial Structure and Social Issues in Urban America* (1975), p. 174.

"The dwelling place shapes the dweller. When all dwellings are the same shape, all dwellers are the same shape."

John Keats
The Crack in the Picture Window

atively recent. Formerly, migration was viewed as a function of what it did to specific areas — cities, suburbs and rural America. Increasingly, concern is being expressed about what all this moving around is doing to the people involved.

Some writers assert that excessive moving has damaging social and emotional side effects. It is argued that moving produces a sense of rootlessness and depersonalization. The average American moves some 14 times during his lifetime, according to Larry H. Long of the Census Bureau. This compares with eight moves per lifetime for Britons and five for Japanese.[12] Author

---

[12] Larry H. Long, "On Measuring Geographic Mobility," *Journal of American Statistical Association*, September 1970, p. 28. See also "Mobility in American Life," *E.R.R.*, 1973 Vol. I, pp. 333-351.

Vance Packard, who identified the American suburbs as a breeding ground for the mobility impulse, has suggested that this mobility has contributed to a national sense of "disconnection." "Great numbers of [suburban] inhabitants feel unconnected to either people or places. . . . Throughout much of the nation . . . in fact, there is a general shattering of small group life. We are confronted with a society that is coming apart at the seams. And in the process we appear to be breeding a legacy of coldness in many of the coming generations."[13]

Herbert J. Gans, the author-sociologist, disagreed. In his classic study of the New Jersey suburb of Levittown, Gans came to the conclusion that suburbia was not as bad as it has been made out to be. Most people who move to the suburbs "are pleased with the community that develops; they enjoy the house and take pleasure from outdoor living and the large supply of compatible people, without experiencing the boredom ascribed to suburban homogeneity." However, Gans added: "Some people encounter unexpected social isolation, particularly those who differ from the majority of their neighbors. . . . The least happy people are always those of the lowest income and the least education; they not only have the most difficulty in making social contacts and joining groups, but are also beset by financial problems which strain family tempers as well as family budgets."[14]

Sociologist Elizabeth Barnett, on the other hand, has cited many positive aspects of mobility. "To suffer loss, to recover from it and go on, fortifies one for living and gives one a deeper sense of oneself. . . . Moving the family can be a time for search and discovery — a time that adds new dimensions and meaning to life."[15]

Evolution of the Outer City

C OLONIAL AMERICA'S urban gentry, seeking seasonal escape from the congestion of their coastal cities, built residences in outlying areas. Some constructed mansions in places such as Harlem, then a village on upper Manhattan Island, or in Dorchester and Roxbury near Boston. Close enough to afford access to commerce and trade, yet far enough away to offer relief from the hurry and disorder of city life, these retreats were the nation's first suburban enclaves.

[13] Vance Packard, *A Nation of Strangers* (1972), p. 8.

[14] Herbert J. Gans, *The Levittowners* (1967), p. 409.

[15] Elizabeth Barnett, *What Moving Means to the Family* (1966), p. 11.

Population Changes in Major Cities

City	1976 est.	1970	Change
New York	7,422,831	7,895,563	− 6.0%
Chicago	3,074,084	3,369,357	− 8.8
Los Angeles	2,743,994	2,811,801	− 2.4
Philadelphia	1,797,403	1,949,996	− 7.8
Houston	1,455,046	1,282,443	13.5
Detroit	1,314,206	1,514,063	−13.2
Dallas	848,829	849,410	− 0.1
Baltimore	827,439	905,787	− 8.7
San Diego	789,059	697,471	13.1
San Antonio	783,765	708,582	10.6
Indianapolis	708,867	729,768	− 2.9
Washington	700,130	756,668	− 7.5
Phoenix	769,512	589,016	15.4
Memphis	667,880	657,007	1.7
San Francisco	663,478	715,674	− 7.3
Milwaukee	661,082	717,372	−.7.9
Cleveland	625,643	750,879	−16.7
Boston	618,250	641,071	− 3.6
New Orleans	580,959	593,471	− 2.1
San Jose	573,806	461,212	24.4

Source: U.S. Bureau of the Census

But large-scale migration out of cities did not start until the onset of vast industrialization and immigration prior to the Civil War. As throngs of new arrivals from Europe settled in the central cities of the East Coast, the resulting social tensions further enhanced the appeal of living in more peaceful surroundings beyond the city. Few of these settlements went as far to preserve their privacy as the suburban communities of St. Louis' West Side, which in the late 1840s erected granite walls and hired a special police force to help keep out undesirables.

The intellectual spirit of the age counseled a suspicion of cities and embraced the pastoral values of the countryside. Indeed, under the influence of such writers as Henry David Thoreau and Ralph Waldo Emerson, many came to favor total removal to the country, believing cities to be, as Thomas Jefferson had advised, places of vice and corruption. Horace Greeley, editor of the *New York Tribune* and a mythologizer of rural America, summarized his era's faith in country living: "Secure to the family the inducements of a home, surrounded by fruits and flowers, rational village movements and sports, the means of education and independence. Get them out of the cities and would-be cities into scenes like those, and the work is done."[16]

---

[16] Horace Greeley, quoted in *Suburbia: The American Dream and Dilemma* (1976), Philip C. Dolce, ed., p. 4.

Improved urban transportation in the 1850s made long-distance commuting feasible for thousands and encouraged greater numbers of city residents to move to the suburbs. Omnibuses in Boston offered six-cent rides from outlying fringes to the downtown "Hub." In 1860, New York City's horse railway system carried over 45 million passengers, transforming nearby villages in Long Island and New Jersey into "bedroom" communities.

The transportation revolution changed the face of urban America. As metropolitan areas expanded to take in older suburban communities, the wealthy retreated still farther into the countryside. Expensive trolley and railway fares, which limited travel to those who could afford it, acted as a kind of selective filter on class movement out of cities. Inner-city districts tended to be settled largely by blue-collar classes, while the suburbs became more and more the domain of the aspiring middle class. At first isolated subdivisions of farmland, these cluster communities gradually meshed together to form "a ring of exclusivity" around many cities, a visible sign of America's emerging hierarchy of mobility and privilege.

By the late 19th century, most large American cities had become socially and economically stratified. The affluent lived in their posh neighborhoods, comfortably segregated from the poor in their economic ghettos. As populations spread, many central cities simply annexed those areas to which the middle class had gravitated. New York, for example, added more than 250 square miles in 1891, and in 1914 Boston doubled its area. Some states established automatic annexation procedures. By 1920, however, political opposition to the absorption of fringe districts mounted and large cities, especially in the congested Northeast, found themselves unable to keep pace, through annexation or consolidation, with suburban migration.

Automobile's Leading Role in Urban Exodus

During the 1920s, general prosperity and the increasing number of automobiles gave new impetus to the growth of the suburbs. In that decade, the suburban populations around the 17 largest U.S. cities rose by nearly 40 percent, while the rate of growth for most cities fell sharply. But until the 1940s, the central city remained almost exclusively the focal point of business and industry; the surrounding suburbs were primarily commuter villages.

After World War II, suburbia began to take on the character of a refuge from the city and its poor. Highways, built largely with federal money, carried ex-urbanites to homes far beyond city limits. The suburbs filled with families moving outward from urban cores and inward from rural regions. Herbert J. Gans wrote that 20th century migration to the suburbs had much in common with the urge that compelled 19th century pioneers to settle the American West. But western settlers were seeking freedom and economic opportunity, while new suburbanites were lured by the promise of comfort: "They were not looking for roots or a rural idyll, not for a social ethic or a consumption-centered life, not for civic participation or for 'sense of community.' They wanted the good or comfortable life for themselves and their families, and the anticipated peacefulness of outdoor living."[17]

In the East and Midwest, the regional shift was particularly dramatic. The five boroughs[18] of New York accounted for 68 percent of the metropolitan area's population in 1910 but only 39 percent in 1970. Cincinnati's share dropped in that time from 63 to 33 percent, Cleveland's from 85 to 36 percent, and Detroit's from 77 to 36 percent. Business and the jobs followed the people to the suburbs. In the 1960s, New York City lost 9.7 percent of its jobs, while its suburbs gained 24.9 percent. For Los Angeles the figures were 10.8 and 16.2, and for Chicago 13.9 and 64.4.[19]

Highways led the outgrowth of suburbs into the countryside. Road construction often precedes urban expansion and makes it inevitable. More than any other single factor, the federal highway program is cited as the main cause of the suburban explosion. The extension of highways determined how land developed and thus how millions of people lived and worked.

Relocating Industry and Jobs to the Suburbs

The movement of industry to the suburbs includes not just factories but corporate offices. Over two dozen of the "Fortune 500" leading industrial companies have moved their headquarters out of New York City in recent years, many of them to the suburbs. According to New York's Regional Planning Association, 2.4 million additional jobs will be created in the metropolitan area by 1985; 2 million of them in the suburbs. Since 1970, 90 percent of the Chicago area's industrial expansion has taken place in the suburbs, along with three-fourths of the residential building and more than one-half of the commercial construction.

The U.S. Bureau of Labor Statistics reports that 90 percent of the jobs in all metropolitan areas since 1960 have been created in the suburbs. The far suburbs, in fact, have emerged as a leading business and industrial zone. Industrial parks and office

---

[17] Herbert J. Gans, *op. cit.,* p. 37.
[18] Manhattan, Brooklyn, Queens, the Bronx and Richmond (Staten Island).
[19] Figures cited by Robert C. Weaver in "The Suburbanization of America," *Civil Rights Digest,* spring 1977, p. 5. Weaver was secretary of housing and urban development in 1966-1968.

clusters have become a common feature of the so-called "outer suburban ring," which some experts now believe to be the "dominant incubator" for the nation's business and manufacturing firms. Many suburbs have become virtually independent of the central cities they surround. Once mere "satellite communities," the suburbs are becoming vast, amorphous, urbanized areas where people live, work, shop and entertain themselves.

The ironic reality of the American flight to suburbia has been that those who were trying to escape brought the city's problems with them. Crime in many suburbs is rising at a higher rate than in central cities. Housing is becoming increasingly expensive and scarce. Traffic congestion and pollution are nearly as bad in some suburban communities as in larger cities. And many suburbs have their share of racial problems, slums, drugs and ennui. Lewis Mumford, one of the nation's most respected urbanologists, has written:

> To withdraw like a hermit and live like a prince — this was the purpose of the original creators of the suburb. This utopia proved to be, up to a point, a realizable one: so enchanting that those who contrived it failed to see the fatal penalty attached to it — the penalty of popularity, the fatal inundation of a mass movement whose numbers would wipe out the goods each individual sought for his own domestic circle, and worse, replace them with a life that was not even cheap counterfeit, but rather grim antithesis.[20]

New Towns: Fading Hope of Another Decade

In the 1960s, the emergence of a few "new towns" was being hailed by many as the potential solution to the problems of urban growth.[21] To the urban planner, frustrated by the complexities of metropolitan growth, a new town was a *tabula rosa*, a clean slate on which to make a fresh start. It was a completely planned community with homes, business and industry, not just a suburban "bedroom community." Many social scientists hoped that such new cities would arrest the spread of the megalopolis; others were less optimistic. Author William H. Whyte wrote toward the end of that decade: "As elements of the metropolis, new towns could not take care of more than a fraction of our future population growth, even under the best of circumstances; nor could they significantly change the structure of the metropolis.[22]

The new towns of the 1930s, called Greenbelt towns,[23] were

---

[20] Lewis Mumford, quoted in *The End of Innocence: A Suburban Reader* (1972), p. 5, Charles Harr, ed.

[21] See "New Towns," *E.R.R.*, 1968 Vol. II, pp. 803-822.

[22] William H. Whyte, *The Last Landscape* (1968), p. 267.

[23] Greenbelt, Md.; Greendale, Wis.; and Greenhills, Ohio. All were built by the Resettlement Administration of the Agriculture Department.

the first publicly assisted, fully planned communities to be built in the United States. During World War II and afterward, the federal government created the "atomic cities" of Los Alamos, N.M., Hanford, Wash., and Oak Ridge, Tenn. But this was an act of military rather than social concern.

The new towns most frequently cited as models for U.S. urban planners, Reston, Va., and Columbia, Md., started rising in the early 1960s with private and corporate financing. In 1968, Congress decided that new towns were socially desirable as a means of developing suburban regions and authorized financial aid for the construction of such communities in Title IV of the Housing and Urban Development Act of that year. Through HUD's New Communities Program, loans have been regulated by the government since 1970 for the development of at least 10 new towns.

The American Institute of Architects (AIA) a decade ago recommended the adoption of a national policy on urban growth and proposed the creation of 100 new communities averaging 100,000 population each and 10 new communities of at least 1,000,000 each. Other proposals suggested that new towns be funded by public corporations and built as a partial solution to the urban growth problem. Although several new communities have been built, the development program has never been as ambitious as once envisioned.

At the dedication of Reston in 1966, Secretary of the Interior Stewart L. Udall said: "A true new town must be a cross-section of America and it must be deemed a failure, despite the brilliance of its design or the insight of community planning . . . if it is an enclave of the well-to-do or the private preserve of a single ethnic or racial group."

In 1974, HUD stopped accepting applications for assistance under its new community program, effectively ending its active involvement in new town development. The government "pullout," many now believe, has doomed the new town concept. Most of the towns that are constructed, wrote *Washington Post* architecture critic Wolf Von Eckardt, turn out to be little more than "ordinary suburban developments," victims of the government's "not so-benign neglect."[24]

Future of Metropolitan U.S.A.

IN MARCH 1978, the Carter administration unveiled its long-awaited urban relief program, a $4 billion aid package to "achieve the revitalization of the nation's cities" and remove

[24] Wolf Von Eckardt, writing in *The Washington Post*, July 7, 1979.

any trace of what President Carter called "anti-urban bias" from the hundreds of federal activities that deal with urban problems.[25] Rather than endorsing a list of social programs, the administration's urban plan stressed long-range economic development for cities by encouraging corporate reinvestment in hard-pressed urban areas.[26]

City officials applauded the Carter initiatives, but lawmakers representing suburban constituencies have said the administration's urban policy discriminates against the suburbs. Especially upsetting to some are the federal government's efforts to lure suburban businesses back to the cities through tax incentives and special reduced-interest loans. Also drawing sharp criticism has been the administration's plan to return to cities many federal facilities now located in the suburbs. "The fact that 40 percent of Americans, the largest such grouping, live in suburban areas is being totally ignored [by the administration]," wrote Rep. Ronald M. Mottl, an Ohio Democrat from suburban Cleveland who is chairman of the Congressional Suburban Caucus. "The proposal pays little attention to the practical necessity of placing federal facilities where people live and work."[27]

Statistics suggest that suburbanites worried about the loss of employment may have cause for concern. Although jobs in the suburbs continued to grow at a faster pace than in the cities, the suburban job-creating ability appeared to taper off early in the 1970s. During the 1960s, employment in suburban centers grew by 18 percent, in contrast to just 4.2 percent in inner cities. But for the first half of this decade, the suburban rate slowed to 5.4 percent, though still far better than in the cities, which experienced a 3.5 percent loss.[28]

"During the 1960s, the suburban centers were outperforming the downtown economies at an extraordinary rate," wrote T. D. Allman, an editor of *Harper's* magazine. "By 1975, though, the situation had changed. . . . Cities began to generate new jobs twice as fast as some of the nearer suburbs, if one takes into account the fact that [these] new jobs are being shared among [a declining urban population of] fewer and fewer people."[29] Voicing similar conclusions, other observers say a suburban employment crisis is not merely on the horizon. In many of the older,

---

[25] White House statement, March 27, 1978.
[26] For background, see "Saving America's Cities," *E.R.R.*, 1977 Vol. II, pp. 869-888.
[27] Letter from Rep. Ronald M. Mottl to the General Services Administration, June 20, 1979.
[28] Rand Corp. analysis of Bureau of Labor Statistics data, cited by T. D. Allman in "Urban Crisis Leaves Town," *Harper's*, November 1978. See also the Rand Corp. study "The Changing Demographic and Economic Structure of Non-metropolitan Areas in the United States," January 1979.
[29] T. D. Allman, "The Urban Crisis Leaves Town," *Harper's*, November 1978, pp. 50-54.

inner suburban areas, where industry is closing and jobs are growing scarce, it has already arrived.

Regional Solutions for Metropolitan Woes

The suburbs of the 1980s are likely to be far different from their predecessors of only a generation ago. Today, most suburban communities are heavily populated "urban" entities. The theory that urban and suburban problems are vastly dissimilar is losing credibility among many experts who are now urging local, state and federal officials to develop regional assistance programs to help cities and their surrounding areas.

State governments, with their enormous power over taxes, land use, highway building, and their administration of federal allocations, may, in fact, prove to be the salvation of many ailing metropolitan areas. In the past, federal and state policies often have worked at cross purposes.

Michigan, under Republican Gov. William G. Milliken, has installed what some observers believe to be a model city-suburbs revenue-sharing program. Michigan now subsidizes services that Detroit and its suburbs use. In addition, the state has enacted a 12-year, tax-benefit plan to encourage the balanced development of factory construction in the Detroit metropolitan area. Despite the opposition of some state legislators representing rural districts, Milliken intends to expand the state assistance program to other cities in Michigan.

In California, legislation enacted in 1977 requires communities to incorporate a mix of moderate- and low-income housing in any future development plans. Also, lawmakers are attempting to revive a bill, defeated two years ago, to conserve open spaces in the path of suburban expansion.

In an effort to coordinate economic growth with the needs of communities, Massachusetts has developed a strategy to aid the fringe areas of both large and small towns, which often suffer the same effects when populations and jobs move away. Massachusetts officials have charged that many states in the past paved the way for housing sprawl and far-flung industrial development by providing interstate highways and access roads to future manufacturing sites "in the middle of nowhere."

A city-suburbs policy similar to the one Massachusetts has adopted could have considerable national appeal. Such a comprehensive approach could save energy and prevent haphazard growth. It might also prove attractive to suburbanites whose communities are now reeling with the explosive development of recent years. The only sacrifice this change in perspective would

Income Range and Residence of Workers

Residence and Income Range	Job Location		
	Central Cities	Suburbs	Non-Metro-politan
Central Cities			
Workers *(in thousands)*	16,338	3,724	784
Income range *(in percent)*			
$3,999 and under	28.8	21.1	19.6
4,000-7,999	26.1	24.6	21.9
8,000-14,999	32.5	38.8	38.1
15,000-24,999	10.2	13.4	16.5
25,000 and over	2.5	2.1	3.7
Suburbs			
Workers *(in thousands)*	8,932	18,001	2,646
Income range *(in percent)*			
$3,999 and under	19.3	30.3	23.0
4,000-7,999	30.5	21.4	17.0
8,000-14,999	26.5	31.2	33.8
15,000-24,999	18.1	13.7	19.6
25,000 and over	5.6	3.3	6.6
Non-Metropolitan Areas			
Workers *(in thousands)*	997	1,090	20,221
Income range *(in percent)*			
$3,999 and under	17.8	20.4	38.3
4,000-7,999	21.7	20.9	26.3
8,000-14,999	41.1	41.7	26.9
15,000-24,999	16.6	15.3	7.2
24,999 and over	2.9	1.7	1.3

Source: Department of Housing and Urban Development, figures for 1975.

require, advocates say, is the abandonment of the need many Americans continue to feel for their long-distance way of life.

Reassessing Further Suburban Expansion

The suburbanization of business and industry, which began after World War II and accelerated in recent years, has reshaped the economic geography of metropolitan America. Once regarded as a retreat from the congestion of urban commerce, the far suburbs have become vast consumer-oriented marketing centers. Increasingly settled by the affluent segment of the population, the magnetic attractions of the outlying suburban ring are the "super-regional" shopping malls. These mammoth self-contained complexes loom as the new hubs of suburban life.

The suburbs have fully matured as the nation's retail pacesetter, drawing both mall-type facilities and corporation headquarters. The people follow as if pulled "by some outward drift" of the commercial tide.[30] The trend toward larger regional shopping malls has been called by promoters one of the most spectacular successes in American enterprise.

But the transforming effect malls have on metropolitan population patterns could reverse that success. The construction of malls and the accompanying rapid development of the distant suburbs portend a "grim scenario," said Neal R. Peirce, a nationally syndicated columnist who writes on the problems of cities. Citing a study by the Michigan Council of Governments on that state's population trends, Peirce predicted: "Unless the last several years' patterns of growth at the suburban fringe are curbed," established urban centers could lose more than "a third of their populations by the end of the century."[31]

The Department of Agriculture has estimated that between 1967 and 1975 24.3 million acres of producing cropland in the United States were lost to development. "Sadly," Peirce wrote, "the best and most endangered farmland tends to be near urban centers." Some counties — notably Suffolk in New York, Howard in Maryland and King in Washington — are making efforts to purchase farm development rights and thus slow commercial sprawl. Effective land-use plans have also been advanced in Honolulu, Minneapolis-St. Paul and Portland, Ore. But the majority of areas have fallen behind these cities in protecting land from suburban development.

While the containment of sprawl may seem to many a worthy objective, it crosses paths with one of the most sacrosanct of all American aspirations — owning a free-standing home of one's own. That is what gave rise to the suburbs in the first place. And before suburban expansion can be brought under control, it may be necessary, as some foresee, for that dream to give up the ghost.

------

[30] Muller, *op. cit.*, p. 32.

[31] Neal R. Peirce, writing in *The Washington Post*, July 11, 1979.

Selected Bibliography

Books

Anderson, Martin, *The Federal Bulldozer: A Critical Analysis of Urban Renewal, 1949-1960*, MIT Press, 1964.

Didion, Joan, *Slouching Towards Bethlehem*, Delta, 1968.

Gans, Herbert J., *The Levittowners: Ways of Life and Politics in a New Suburban Community*, Penguin, 1967.

Dolce, Philip C., ed., *Suburbia: The American Dream and Dilemma*, Anchor/Doubleday, 1976.

Lynd, Robert S. and Helen M. Lynd, *Middletown*, Harcourt, Brace, 1959.

——*Middletown in Transition: A Study in Cultural Conflicts*, Harcourt, Brace, 1963.

Jacobs, Jane, *The Economy of Cities*, Random House, 1969.

Mumford, Lewis, *The Urban Prospect*, Harcourt, Brace, 1968.

——*The Highway and the City*, Harcourt, Brace, 1963.

Raban, Jonathan, *Soft City: The Art of Cosmopolitan Living*, Dutton, 1974.

Stanback, Thomas M. and Robert V. Knight, *Suburbanization and the City*, Osmun & Co., 1978.

Articles

Allman, T. D., "The Urban Crisis Leaves Town," *Harper's*, December 1978.

Nation's Cities, selected issues.

"St. Louis: A Dying City Bounces Back," *U.S. News & World Report*, July 23, 1979.

Taeuber, Conrad, "A Changing America," *American Demographics*, January 1979.

Warner, Edwin, "Suburbia's Gift to the Cities," *Horizon*, September 1977.

Weaver, Robert C., "The Suburbanization of America," *Civil Rights Digest*, spring 1977.

Will, George, "Levittown Revisited," *Newsweek*, July 1979.

Williams, Roger M., "The Assault on Fortress Suburbia: How Long Can the Poor Be Kept Out?" *Saturday Review*, Feb. 18, 1978.

Reports and Studies

American Academy of Political and Social Science, "The Suburban Seventies," November 1970.

Editorial Research Reports, "New Towns," 1968 Vol. II, p. 812; "Restrictions on Urban Growth," 1973 Vol. I, p. 87; "Housing Outlook," 1977 Vol. I, p. 289; "Housing Restoration and Displacement," 1978 Vol. II, p. 861.

Suburban Action Institute, "Open or Closed Suburbs: Corporate Location and the Urban Crisis," 1970.

U.S. Bureau of the Census, "Social and Economic Characteristics of Metropolitan and Nonmetropolitan Areas, 1977 and 1970," Special Studies P-23 No. 75, issued November 1978.

——"Population Profile of the United States: 1978," Series P-20 No. 336, issued April 1979.

U.S. Department of Justice, "Crime in the United States, 1977," October 1978.

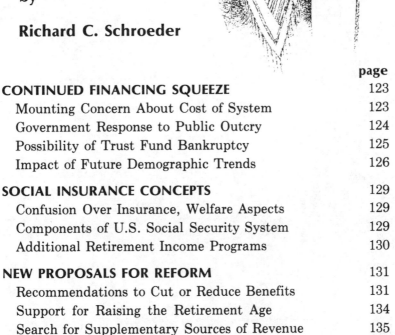

Social Security Reassessment

by

Richard C. Schroeder

June 29
1 9 7 9

SOCIAL SECURITY REASSESSMENT

BEGINNING in July, Social Security recipients will get a 9.9 percent increase in benefits to offset recent rises in the cost of living. The increase, the largest since Congress authorized automatic inflation adjustments in 1972, will add $10.2 billion to the Social Security retirement and disability tab, now running at nearly $100 billion a year.[1] Although the rise in benefits will not entail any increase in Social Security taxes beyond those already mandated by law, it is likely to add fuel to the mounting taxpayers' revolt over the payroll tax bite.

Congress in 1977 approved steep increases in both Social Security tax rates and in the wage levels on which the tax is paid, to take effect between 1979 and 1990 *(see box p. 127)*. As a result, Social Security taxes will more than double for most middle and upper income workers in the next five years. Many low-income families already are paying more in Social Security than in income tax. The same will hold true for an increasing number of middle-income families during the 1980s.

Congress is clearly uneasy about the political impact of the payroll tax hikes. The legislators are torn between a desire to keep Social Security contributions within reasonable bounds, and the need to keep the system from floundering financially. Each year since 1975, the Social Security program has paid out more to beneficiaries than it has collected in taxes. Before the 1977 increases were approved, government actuaries warned that deficits would mount and could bankrupt the system within a few years. The 1977 law improved, but did not completely solve, the financing problem. Experts believe the system will begin posting surpluses in 1981. But revenues will start falling short of costs by 2015 — shortly after the "baby boom" generation starts reaching retirement age *(see p. 126)*.

The general public is, if anything, more uncertain than Congress about the future of Social Security. A Louis Harris survey taken last August and released by the House Committee on Aging in February indicated that two-fifths of American workers have "hardly any confidence at all" that the system will be able

---

[1] This figure does not include health insurance benefits paid under the Medicare program, which also is funded from Social Security payroll taxes. Medicare payments in 1979 will total $21.4 billion and will rise to an estimated $40.5 billion by 1984.

to pay them the benefits they have earned. The commissioner of Social Security, Stanford Ross, agrees that lack of faith in the system is a real threat to its future. "We never paid much attention to the people whose taxes finance the program," he said recently. "We were all caught up in helping beneficiaries."[2]

Many people are not aware of the correlation between Social Security taxes and future benefits. A study prepared for the American Enterprise Institute in 1977 said there was "a vast and imbalanced ignorance about the fiscal details" of the program. "Most workers neither know their current payroll taxes nor display much interest in their future benefits," the study said. "On the other hand, most beneficiaries are ignorant of their past tax 'contributions,' but show a keen interest in their benefits. The political implications of such unbalanced information are powerful and predictable."[3]

Government Response to Public Outcry

Mindful of the "political implications," Congress legislated an income tax cut for this year to offset the payroll tax increases, but balked at demands for a complete revision of the Social Security law. Now even congressional leaders are voicing concern about the political impact of the tax increases mandated by the 1977 amendments, especially the substantial rise due in 1981 *(see box p. 127)*. Hoping to avert at least some of the 1981 rate hike, lawmakers are considering a wide range of options, including reducing benefits, completely overhauling the present financing system, reorganizing the benefit structure and bringing federal employees into the system for the first time.[4]

The chairman of the House Ways and Means Committee, Al Ullman, D-Ore., has pledged to begin hearings on the entire Social Security question sometime this summer or fall. So far this session, 120 members of Congress have introduced amendments to the Social Security Act. President Carter has proposed his own legislative program, which would eliminate a number of Social Security benefits *(see p. 131)*.

Members of Congress are not the only ones in Washington considering the Social Security dilemma. Two study commissions are at work in the Department of Health, Education and Welfare. In addition, a presidentially appointed Commission on Pension Policy is scheduled to deliver a report on the changing

---

[2] Quoted by syndicated columnist Jane Bryant Quinn in *The Washington Post*, May 21, 1979.

[3] William C. Mitchell, "The Popularity of Social Security: A Paradox in Public Choice," American Enterprise Institute, 1977, p. 3.

[4] See Christopher Conte's "Financing Squeeze Forces New Assessment of Social Security," *Congressional Quarterly Weekly Report*, March 17, 1979, pp. 442-449.

role of private retirement programs by 1981. A nine-member National Commission on Social Security, created by the 1977 Social Security amendments, is studying the financial condition of the retirement, disability and health insurance programs, as well as program coverage, benefit levels, inequities, and co-ordination with related government programs. It will present its findings to the president in 1981.

It still is not clear what direction Congress will take on Social Security in coming months. But it seems almost inevitable that Social Security will be an important issue in the 1980 presidential campaign. John Connally, the former governor of Texas who is an announced candidate for the Republican nomination, told the National Federation of Independent Businesses on June 12 that he believed there must be a comprehensive overhaul of the Social Security system "so that its promises do not prove hollow and so that the burden of supporting it does not prove mortal to the labor-intensive small firms."

Possibility of Trust Fund Bankruptcy

Unlike private insurance and pension funds, which depend on actuarially determined reserves for current income, the Social Security system is funded on a pay-as-you-go basis. Benefits to pensioners, survivors and the disabled are paid out of taxes collected from workers. The three Social Security Trust Funds — Old Age and Survivors, Disability, and Health — are reserves held to cover deficits when benefits exceed income in any given year. When and if the trust funds run out, deficits must be made up from other sources, such as general treasury funds, or special taxes.

There has been continuing concern about the possibility that one or more of the trust funds could be depleted as benefits outrun tax collections.[5] The 1977 amendments to the Social Security Act appear to have checked the erosion of the trust funds, at least for the time being. Current projections by the Social Security Administration indicate that the OASI trust fund will shrink to a low level of $22.5 billion in 1980 and then begin to increase, reaching a level of $42.5 billion in 1984.[6] The surplus is projected to continue through the end of this century, as taxes rise slightly faster than benefits. But during the first quarter of the next century, deficits will begin climbing again. To cover the projected shortall the Social Security tax rate would have to be increased by 1.11 percentage points. To meet projected costs in the years 2025 to 2050, the tax rate would have to be increased by 4.11 percentage points.

---

[5] See, for example, "Social Security Financing," *E.R.R.*, 1972 Vol. II, pp. 705-724.

[6] Source: Working paper of the National Commission on Social Security.

The problem for Congress and Social Security planners is to determine how much of a payroll tax bite workers can sustain, and at what point political reverberations will put the entire system in jeopardy. In the next five years, payroll taxes will more than double. By 1984 the maximum Social Security tax paid by employees will climb to $2,472 compared to $1,071 in 1978. For self-employed persons, the maximum tax will go from $1,435 in 1978 to $3,450 in 1984. Yearly increases are built into the system through the middle of the next century, with the biggest increases affecting middle- and upper-income workers. Understandably, some experts liken Social Security financing to a time bomb, set to go off in the next fifty years.[7]

Impact of Future Demographic Trends

Current projections for Social Security trust fund balances could be skewed by future economic developments. A prolonged recession, with high unemployment, would cut into payroll tax collections, without significantly reducing benefits. Accelerated inflation, on the other hand, would push benefits still higher, since pensions are indexed to wages. Congress could, of course, alter such trends by increasing or reducing benefits or taxes. In the long run, however, it seems virtually certain that the costs of the Social Security system will continue to spiral, exceeding the growth in wages, prices and productivity. The reasons are demographic — changes in the age composition of the American people.

The average life span of Americans has increased nearly ten years since the first Social Security benefits were paid in 1940. Life expectancy is now 69 years for men and 77 years for women, and will increase by at least three more years by the middle of the next century. About 10 percent of the U.S. population (22.4 million people) is now 65 or older. In the next 50 years, that proportion will more than double to 22 percent. By comparison, barely four percent of the population was 65 or over at the turn of this century.[8]

The bulk of the Social Security load now is being carried by the generation born during the low-fertility years of the 1930s. When these men and women, now in their forties, reach retirement age toward the end of the century, their smaller numbers will mean a lower pension burden. The wage-earning group then will be made up of those born during the post-war "baby boom" of the late 1940s and 1950s. For a brief period, the system will be

---

[7] See, for example, comments of W. Allen Wallis, Chancellor of the University of Rochester, in "The Future of the Social Security System," printed proceedings of a Roundtable discussion sponsored by the American Enterprise Institute, Oct. 27, 1977, p. 10.

[8] Roy Lubove, *The Struggle for Social Security 1900-1935* (1968), p. 114.

Social Security Tax Schedule

Years	Maximum taxable earnings	Combined payroll tax rate[a]	Maximum tax
1937-49	$ 3,000	1.0 %	$ 30.00
1950	3,000	1.5	45.00
1951-53	3,600	1.5	54.00
1954	3,600	2.0	72.00
1955-56	4,200	2.0	84.00
1957-58	4,200	2.25	94.50
1959	4,800	2.5	120.00
1960-61	4,800	3.0	144.00
1962	4,800	3.125	150.00
1963-65	4,800	3.625	174.00
1966	6,600	4.2	277.20
1967	6,600	4.4	290.40
1968	7,800	4.4	343.20
1969	7,800	4.8	374.40
1970	7,800	4.8	374.40
1971	7,800	5.2	405.60
1972	9,000	5.2	468.00
1973	10,800	5.85	631.80
1974	13,200	5.85	772.20
1975	14,100	5.85	824.85
1976	15,300	5.85	895.05
1977	16,500	5.85	965.25
1978	17,700	6.05	1,070.85
1979	22,900	6.13	1,403.77
1980	25,900	6.13	1,587.67
1981	29,700	6.65	1,975.05
1982	31,800	6.70	2,130.60
1983	33,900[b]	6.70	2,271.30[c]
1984	36,000[b]	6.70	2,412.00[c]
1985	38,100[b]	7.05	2,686.05[c]
1986	40,200[b]	7.15	2,874.30[c]
1987	42,600[b]	7.15	3,045.90[c]

a. Employee and employer, each. Combined tax rate includes retirement, survivors, disability and hospital insurance programs.

b. Estimates based on an automatic adjustment mechanism that increases the wage base as incomes increase.

c. Dependent on maximum taxable earnings (see note b).

SOURCE: Social Security Administration

in relative balance. But when the "baby boom" becomes the "senior boom," about the year 2015, the number of aged will rise dramatically. By 2030, there will be an estimated 55 million retired Americans.

The members of the "baby boom" generation have produced a "baby bust." The average fertility rate, which stood at 3.8 children per woman in 1957, has plummeted to 1.7 children today. There will be far fewer workers in the "baby bust" generation to support the coming "senior boom" in the next century. Other factors will complicate the problem. For a number of reasons people are living longer, but retiring earlier. Three decades ago, nearly half of all men 65 and over remained in the work force. Today, only one man in five and one woman in twelve work after reaching age 65.

The net result of these trends is to push sharply upward the dependency ratio — the relationship between non-productive citizens and the workers who must support them. In 1900, there were less than 10 retired persons for each 100 workers.[9] By 1975, 30 persons were receiving Social Security benefits for each 100 workers. According to several projections, the ratio will climb to 50 retired persons per 100 workers by the year 2025, or one Social Security beneficiary for each 2 workers.[10]

The wild card in these projections is the continuing influx of illegal immigrants into the United States. No one knows exactly how many undocumented persons are entering the country each year. According to some estimates, illegal immigrants together with the 400,000 annual legal immigrants, now account for 50 percent or more of U.S. population growth. Since immigrants tend to be younger than the population as a whole, many of the illegals still will be in the work force when the "baby boom" generation retires. Provided the immigrants obtain high enough paid jobs, there is the possibility that "a large, mostly white, retired group would be supported by a relatively small, disproportionately foreign-born working population."[11]

The Social Security Act makes no distinction between persons working legally or illegally in this country; both can qualify for retirement, disability and survivors' benefits. A large proportion of illegal aliens — between 65 and 90 percent, according to one estimate — have Social Security and income taxes deducted from their paychecks.[12] An upcoming study by the U.S. General Accounting Office indicates that the Social Security entitlements of illegal aliens could represent a significant drain on the system in the future.

[9] *Pension Facts 1976,* American Council of Life Insurance, 1977, p. 37.

[10] See, for example, June A. O'Neill, "Future Financing of the System," in *Financing Social Security* (1979), Colin D. Campbell, ed., p. 175.

[11] Harrison H. Donnelly, "Aging U.S. Population Poses Threat to Retirement Systems," *Congressional Quarterly Weekly Report,* March 17, 1979, p. 441.

[12] Douglas S. Massey, "Hordes of Illegals? No," *The New York Times,* May 31, 1979. Massey is a research associate in the Office of Population Research at Princeton University.

Social Insurance Concepts

SOCIAL Security originally was conceived as "social insurance," a government risk-assuming venture to guarantee replacement of income lost through retirement, disability or death. There was to be a direct relationship between paid-in contributions and benefits received. Over the years, however, greater emphasis has been placed on assuring an adequate retirement income to all participants. Distribution of benefits has been weighted toward the lower end of the income scale so that, proportionately, lower paid workers have more of their working-life income "replaced" than do higher paid employees. "The Social Security system today is a far cry from the limited 'insurance' plan adopted in the 1930s," according to a paper prepared for the Joint Economic Committee of Congress. "It has become a gigantic tax system aimed at redistributing income from workers to retirees, more and more on the basis of 'need' and less and less on the basis of past contributions."[13]

On the other hand, Social Security is not strictly a welfare program, based solely on the concept of "social adequacy." Although the ratio between contributions and benefits is not fixed, the benefit formulas have at least a partial actuarial basis; that is, there remains a rudimentary connection between individual input and benefits. The notion that Social Security is a tax, like the income tax, is dismissed by both critics and defenders of the system. An income tax is uniformly applied to all; but 10 percent of American wage earners are exempt from Social Security contributions. Moreover, much of the congressional resistance to funding Social Security deficits from general treasury revenues *(see p. 135)* stems from the fear that the system would then be seen as "just another tax."

Components of U.S. Social Security System

The primary and oldest elements of the Social Security system are the Old Age, Survivors and Disability Insurance programs. The programs are designed to be self-supporting and are funded through a year-to-year transfer of income between generations. Each is backed by a reserve trust fund to cover deficits in fund-short years. In 1965 the OASDI trust funds were joined by a Health Insurance trust fund, tied to Medicare, a health insurance program for persons 65 years and older. A companion program, Medicaid, was legislated to provide health care for the poor from public funds. Medicare is funded on the same pay-as-

---

[13] "Issues in Financing Retirement Income," Paper No. 18 in *Studies in Public Welfare,* Joint Economic Committee of Congress, Dec. 27, 1974, p. 93.

you-go principle as Social Security, while Medicaid legitimately can be classified as a welfare program. The Social Security Administration administered the Medicare program until 1977, when it was transferred to a newly created Health Care Financing Administration (HCFA) in the Department of Health, Education and Welfare. Social Security field offices still perform certain routine administrative functions for Medicare.[14]

Over the years, Congress and successive administrations have given the Social Security Administration responsibility for managing a variety of welfare-type programs, which are not financed by payroll taxes but from general revenues. Part of the public's confusion about the nature of Social Security arises from the mingling of responsibility for OASDI trust funds and income-test programs. Among the welfare programs administered by the Social Security Administration are Supplemental Security Income (SSI),[15] the Black Lung program for miners and Aid to Families With Dependent Children (AFDC).

In addition to these programs, the Social Security Administration has other minor social program responsibilities. Field offices assist in enforcement of child support laws and in locating absent parents. SSA manages special assistance programs for Cuban and Indochinese refugees and it has certain intake responsibilities for the food stamp program of the Department of Agriculture.

Additional Retirement Income Programs

Social Security planners speak of a "four-level approach to income security for the elderly."[16] These comprise, in addition to Social Security, private and public pension systems, individual savings, and various federal and state welfare programs. Of these, the latter provide the least significant portion of retirement income (although for many individuals they may mean the difference between moderate security and despair). While 90 percent of all persons 65 and over receive Social Security benefits, only 8 to 9 percent receive Supplemental Security Income. Additional support for the needy aged may come from the Medicaid and food stamp programs.

Private and public pension plans play an important role in supplementing Social Security, a fact recognized by the tax-

---

[14] See "Medicare and Medicaid After Ten Years," *E.R.R.*, 1975 Vol. II, p. 523.

[15] Congress in 1974 merged existing federal-state cooperative programs of assistance to the aged, the blind and the permanently disabled into SSI. The program guarantees minimum incomes to recipients to bring them up to or near the poverty level.

[16] Robert M. Ball, "Income Security for the Elderly," *National Journal*, Oct. 28, 1978, p. 1748.

deferred status of private plans, and by the existence of federal regulatory legislation — the Employment Retirement Security Income Act (ERISA) — which establishes minimum standards for private pension fund management. Altogether, there are about 500,000 corporate pension plans, with assets totaling close to $300 billion.[17] The 96th Congress is studying major changes in ERISA to protect workers against defaults and mismanagement. Self-employed persons may establish their own retirement plans (the so-called HR 10, or Keogh Plans) and workers not covered by a company pension plan may set up Individual Retirement Accounts. Both plans are tax-deferred. According to the American Council of Life Insurance, more than $6 billion is invested in such accounts today.

One-fourth of the federal budget is spent on programs for the aged. Some experts think the proportion could rise to 40 percent early in the next century. Even at this level of spending, however, it is clear that Social Security is not and cannot be the entire answer to income security for the retired. The question is: how well does the four-level mosaic of public and private programs do the job of providing for the retirement years? The answer appears to be: rather poorly. Studies indicate that at least 25 percent of the aging, or 5.5 million people, lack sufficient income to maintain a minimum adequate permanent diet.[18] Of these, at least 3.3 million live at or below the poverty threshold.[19] In 1976, only 20 percent of the aged benefited from private pension plans; 13 percent received government employee pensions (compared with the 90 percent who receive Social Security income).[20]

New Proposals for Reform

PRESIDENT CARTER, in his proposed budget for fiscal year 1980, urged Congress to eliminate a number of "unnecessary" Social Security benefits. That the president would even mention the possibility of reducing benefits reflects a profound shift in thinking about Social Security. Since the program's

---

[17] Martin Donsky, "Congress Opens New Debate on Private Pension System," *Congressional Quarterly Weekly Report,* March 17, 1979, p. 450.

[18] Robert H. Binstock, "Federal Policy Toward the Aging — Its Inadequacies and its Politics," *National Journal,* Nov. 11, 1978, p. 1839.

[19] The official Federal Poverty Threshold for a couple aged 65 or older in 1979 was $4,270 a year. However, new research by Mollie Orshansky, a statistician for the Social Security Administration who helped in developing the original concepts related to poverty lines, suggests that a more realistic threshold would be $5,920.

[20] Source: Working Paper of the National Commission on Social Security.

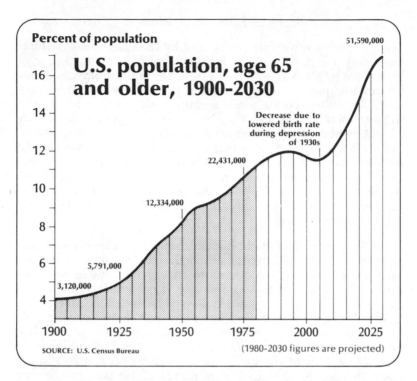

Percent of population

U.S. population, age 65 and older, 1900-2030

51,590,000

Decrease due to lowered birth rate during depression of 1930s

22,431,000

12,334,000

5,791,000

3,120,000

1900   1925   1950   1975   2000   2025

SOURCE: U.S. Census Bureau   (1980-2030 figures are projected)

inception, Congress has done little but increase benefits. Among the changes Carter proposed was a phaseout of education benefits for dependent children over age 18. The administration argued that the student benefit was actually an education stipend, more appropriately made through HEW's programs of educational grants and loans.

Spouses caring for children of retired, disabled or deceased workers currently may receive immediately benefits they would not normally get until they reach age 60 or 62. Carter wants to cut off surviving parent benefits after the youngest child reaches age 16. The president also recommended eliminating the present law provision guaranteeing insured workers who retire at age 65 $120 a month regardless of their past earnings. He called the provision a "windfall" to persons for whom Social Security covered employment is not the principal source of pre-retirement earnings.[21]

The House Ways and Means Committee, on April 9, approved an administration-supported bill that would save the federal government an estimated $1 billion a year by changing the Social Security disability insurance program. The bill, which was cleared for floor action by the House Rules Committee June 7, is intended to encourage people to go back to work by making

---

[21] For a complete list of Carter's proposed changes in Social Security benefits see *Congressional Quarterly Weekly Report*, Jan. 27, 1979, pp. 122-123.

benefit status less attractive. Under the bill, workers who qualify for disability insurance after Jan. 1, 1980, would receive no more than 80 percent of their prior average monthly earnings. Total family payments would be limited to 150 percent of the worker's basic individual benefit. A beneficiary gets extra cash for supporting a dependent spouse and children.

The bill contained several provisions aimed at giving the disabled extra help in getting out of the program. Recognizing that disabled persons sometimes find it difficult to go back to work, the bill extended the "trial work period" now allowed to job returnees. Under existing law, a returnee gets benefits for nine months after going back to work; after that he or she has to reapply for benefits should work prove impossible. Under the bill approved by the Ways and Means Committee, a returnee would receive benefits for a full year. More important, the bill would allow those who were unsuccessful in their attempt to get work to get back on the program immediately, within two years of leaving it, without having to reapply.[22]

President Carter's plan for a $24 billion national health insurance program also could have an impact on Social Security costs and benefits. Carter's health scheme, which was sent to Congress on June 12, seeks $18.2 billion in new federal spending, and additional employer contributions of $6.1 billion to protect workers against catastrophic illness expenses. Under the Carter plan, employee contributions, which form part of the over-all Social Security payroll tax, could rise as much as $1.7 billion a year. But according to the president, the tax increases would be offset by savings on medical bills. Congress also is considering a health insurance proposal introduced by Sen. Edward M. Kennedy, D-Mass.

There is some support in Congress for changing the formulas by which Social Security benefits are indexed. The current system, called "wage indexing," provides for automatic adjustments in benefits to match the growth in wages. That in effect increases benefits for retirees to keep pace with both inflation and the increasing productivity of the work force. Some people argue that retirees should not benefit from productivity improvements by current workers. They propose switching to "price indexing," which would enable retirement benefits to keep pace with inflation only. The change from wage to price indexing would produce relatively small savings initially, but over the long run it could be sufficient to cut the payroll tax rate 3.7 percentage points.[23]

---

[22] See *Congressional Quarterly Weekly Report*, April 14, 1979, pp. 691-694.

[23] See Robert S. Kaplan, "Indexing Social Security," American Enterprise Institute, 1977.

Congress took a modest step toward reducing Social Security expenditures in 1977 when it corrected a technical deficiency that actually overcompensated Social Security beneficiaries for inflation. To correct the problem, Congress separated or "decoupled" the process of granting cost of living increases to already retired persons from the computation of initial benefit levels for future retirees. Benefits, once awarded, still may be increased to compensate for inflation, but the benefit structure used for post-retirement computations will not increase.[24]

Support for Raising the Retirement Age

A number of economists and politicians have argued that raising the age of eligibility for Social Security to 68 or older would resolve much of the financial problem.[25] North Carolina State University economist Robert L. Clark told the House Select Committee on Population in 1978 that Congress should consider phasing in over a 20-year period an increase in the retirement age. Under Clark's proposal, the retirement age would be pushed back three months every year, beginning in 1990. That way, it would reach 70 by the year 2010, just when higher taxes would be needed to pay for the retiring baby boom generation.

Those who advocate raising the retirement age argue that 65 is an arbitrary limit, set in a time when life expectancy was considerably different from what it is today. Some adjustment is called for, they maintain, to reflect increasing longevity and the improved health of the aged. Congress last year raised the mandatory retirement age for most private sector workers to 70 and abolished it entirely for federal employees.

Plans to cut Social Security benefits face strong opposition from groups representing the interests of the elderly. Former Health, Education and Welfare Secretary Wilbur E. Cohen, who heads a coalition of elderly and other groups called Save Our Security, believes that cutting benefits would amount to a breach of faith with today's workers and could seriously undermine support for the Social Security system. One problem in cutting benefits is that there is little agreement about whether the current level of benefits is adequate. For more than half of America's retirees, Social Security is the sole source of old-age income. Experts generally believe that retired people need be-

---

[24] The decoupling amendment produced another problem, the so-called "notch" effect, by which persons reaching 62 before 1979 (the year the amendment took effect) will realize substantially higher benefits than those who reach 62 in 1980 and beyond, particularly if the former continue to work until 65 or older. Social Security experts are working on new legislation to correct the notch effect. See the Report to the President and Congress of the National Commission on Social Security, May 11, 1979.

[25] See "The Retirement Incentive of Social Security," *The Socioeconomic Newsletter,* September 1978, pp. 1-3.

tween 60 and 80 percent of their regular wages when they retire. The percentage of pre-retirement income provided by Social Security ranges from 60 percent for low-income workers to 30 percent for high-income workers.

Search for Supplementary Sources of Revenue

Reluctant to cut Social Security benefits, but eager to meet taxpayers' demands for lower payroll deductions, federal lawmakers are searching for new sources of revenue for the Social Security system. Rep. Richard Gebhardt, D-Mo., has proposed raising federal excise taxes on cigarettes and liquor, with the revenues earmarked for Social Security. Congress also is considering a plan to tax all or some Social Security benefits.[26] One of the most common ideas for revising the Social Security system involves using general revenues raised by income and corporate taxes to pay for part of the system's costs.

There are many variations of the general revenue idea. Some would require general revenues to pay a certain percentage of Social Security costs. Others would provide general revenue financing of certain benefit programs, such as health insurance or disability insurance. Still others would use general revenues to cover the costs of benefits for low-income persons. President Carter has proposed using income taxes to supplement the payroll tax whenever high unemployment reduces the income of the Social Security trust funds. A variety of general revenue financing proposals was considered by the House Ways and Means Committee last year, but none was approved.

General revenue financing would not reduce the costs of Social Security. It would merely shift the burden of financing benefits from the payroll tax to other taxes. Advocates argue that would be less burdensome and more progressive, since the progressive income tax makes up a large proportion of the federal government's revenue. Almost all industrial nations use some general revenues to pay for social insurance, but the idea has been difficult to sell in the U.S. Congress. The traditional conservative argument against general revenue financing is that it would undermine the insurance side of Social Security by breaking the link between contributions and benefits.

The primary drawback to all the general-revenue proposals is that "there aren't any extra general funds, just a general-fund deficit," Senate Finance Committee Chairman Russell B. Long, D-La., said recently.[27] Long and other critics of the proposals

---

[26] See Leonard M. Greene, "Social Security Benefits Should Be Taxed," *The Christian Science Monitor*, April 18, 1979. Dr. Greene is president of the Institute for Socioeconomic Studies in White Plains, N.Y.

[27] Quoted in *The Wall Street Journal*, June 8, 1979.

argue that any resort to the Treasury's general fund, without an income tax boost, would swell the deficit, estimated at about $35 billion for the fiscal year ending Sept. 30. Many people see the growing deficit as one of the chief culprits in inflation.

Sen. Long and Rep. Al Ullman have suggested meeting future Social Security costs with a new tax, called the "value-added tax." VAT, as it is known, is essentially a national sales tax, levied on manufacturers at each level of the production and distribution process. European countries long have used such taxes as supplementary financing devices. Supporters of a VAT argue that it is the least painful way of collecting money because it is hidden in the cost of things people buy.

The chief argument against a VAT is that it is inflationary, since it adds directly to the cost of everything. Congressional liberals complain that taxes on consumption hurt the poor, who consume more of their income than do the rich. Fiscal conservatives suspect that Congress would not use a VAT to replace existing taxes, but instead would add another layer to Americans' already heavy tax burden. Moreover, state and local governments worry that a VAT would encroach on their use of sales taxes, the fastest-growing source of state and local revenues.

Extension of Coverage to Government Workers

Additional money could be brought into the system by extending coverage to the 2.8 million federal employees and 3.5 million state and local workers not now participating in Social Security. While most of the extra revenue eventually would be paid out in benefits, "universal coverage" would greatly increase the system's cash flow in the short run. Universal coverage also is seen as a solution to "double-dipping" by a large number of federal employees who qualify for Social Security benefits on top of their lucrative civil service pensions. More than 500,000 civil service beneficiaries are expected in fiscal year 1980 to draw Social Security benefits on top of their pensions. Some will do so by moonlighting in Social Security-covered jobs. Others will qualify because they took advantage of the opportunity to retire from their government jobs when they reached age 55 and then worked in private sector jobs until they could qualify for Social Security.

Legislating universal coverage could be difficult. Federal workers comprise a formidable Washington lobby with ready access to Capitol Hill. And in their view they have something to lobby for — a retirement system that is generally superior to Social Security. Government workers can retire at age 55 after 30 years of service, as compared to the 65-year retirement age under Social Security. In contrast to most private pension plans, they receive automatic cost-of-living increases twice a year. And their benefit levels generally are much higher than Social Security or most private pension systems.

Civil service employees might be persuaded to accept a merger of the retirement systems if Social Security could be used to supplement certain coverage gaps in their own plans. In civil service, for example, survivor benefits are optional; if a government worker elects to provide after-death protection for his dependents, his own pension is correspondingly reduced. A surviving spouse receives a civil service annuity only if the worker has elected the survivor's option, or if he dies while still in government service. In either case, the spouse's benefit is only 55 percent of the full worker benefit.[28] The extension of family benefits under Social Security could actually broaden and strengthen civil service coverage.

For equity and political reasons a merger of the pension systems would have to guarantee retirees as much protection as the present civil service system. The General Accounting Office has proposed four alternative methods for merging the systems, ranging from a "fully additive approach," in which all entitlements of both systems are maintained, to a "complementary approach," under which coverage gaps in each system would be filled in by provisions of the other. Rep. Joseph Fisher, D-Va., has proposed adoption of a "grandfather" clause to permit current government workers to stay out of the Social Security program; only new employees would be covered by the merged plans.

Inequities in System for Women and Others

Recent assessments of Social Security financing problems have illuminated other inequities in the system. A frequently criticized aspect of the system is the so-called "retirement test," which penalizes workers who continue earning salaries after they have qualified for Social Security benefits.[29] Under the retirement test formula, workers lose one dollar of Social Security income for every two dollars earned beyond an "exempt amount." In 1979 retirees over 65 may earn up to $4,500 without losing Social Security benefits. The exempt amount will rise to $5,000 in 1980, $5,500 in 1981 and $6,000 in 1982.[30]

Critics of the retirement test rule argue that it most adversely affects workers near the bottom of the Social Security scale who are generally most in need of additional income from full or

---

[28] *Need for Overall Policy and Coordinated Management of Federal Retirement Systems,* Vol. I, General Accounting Office, Dec. 29, 1978, p. 189.
[29] See Warren Shore, *Social Security: The Fraud in Your Future* (1975), pp. 121-122.
[30] Exempt amounts are proportionately lower for retirees under age 65. The earnings limitation does not apply to disabled workers.

part-time jobs. The retirement test applies only to earned income and not to income from investments or other pension plans, a provision that also appears to favor those in the higher income brackets. Those who defend the retirement test formula argue that Social Security is an "insurance" system. To permit a beneficiary to receive unlimited earned income, they say, would transform Social Security into a pension plan, while to apply an "economic need" test would transform it into a welfare system.

Various categories of workers complain that the Social Security system is inequitable. Single persons argue that they have to pay taxes to the Old Age and Survivors Insurance Trust Fund even though they do not expect to benefit from the survivor provisions. Self-employed persons pay an OASI tax that is 50 percent higher than that paid by salaried employees, although the benefits received by both are the same.[31] Some of the most glaring inequities in the Social Security system apply to women. Under the current system, which has not changed much in 40 years, married women generally receive Social Security protection as dependents of their husbands. If women do work, they can be covered as dependents of their husbands or on their own right, but not both. Should the marriage end in divorce, the woman would lose Social Security protection if the marriage lasted less than 10 years. Widowed homemakers under age 60 cannot receive benefits unless they are either at least age 50 and disabled or caring for children.

Because married women cannot receive both spouse and worker benefits, the protection they receive as workers often duplicates rather than supplements the protection they receive as spouses. In addition, benefits are often higher for couples where one spouse earned most or all of the income than for couples where both spouses had roughly equal earnings, even though the total family earnings in both cases are the same. "On the whole, when both marriage partners work they get somewhat less for their money than if all the wages are earned by one person," former Social Security Commissioner Robert M. Ball has acknowledged.[32] Ball noted, however, that the problem is not one of sex discrimination, but of differential treatment of couples. He added that the two-income family does, in fact, draw greater benefits since dependents are protected in the case of death or disability of either spouse. Furthermore, one spouse can elect for early retirement, drawing Social Security benefits while the other spouse continues to work.

---

[31] The Social Security Administration points out that self-employed persons actually pay only 75 percent of the combined employer-employee tax for the same benefits.

[32] Robert M. Ball, "Income Security for the Elderly," *National Journal*, Oct. 28, 1978, p. 1751.

A study completed by the Department of Health, Education and Welfare last February recommended several changes in the Social Security system to make it more equitable for women. First, it said Congress could require that 50 percent of the total annual earnings of a couple be credited to each spouse's individual earnings record. The benefits of each spouse then would be based on one-half of the couple's earnings during years of marriage and on individual earnings while unmarried. "The idea underlying earnings sharing," the report said, "is that each spouse is an equal partner in marriage and each — whether a worker in paid employment or an unpaid homemaker — should have equal credit for total family earnings." Alternatively, the study said a two-tier benefit system could be established. Everyone would qualify for a flat-dollar benefit, regardless of earnings. In addition, an earnings-related benefit would be payable on the basis of earnings from covered employment.

Despite its problems, financial and otherwise, Social Security remains one of the most popular programs ever enacted by the U.S. government. Over the past 40 years it has paid an estimated $1 trillion to millions of aged, widowed, orphaned, sick and disabled. It has eased the retirement years of many who otherwise would have been destitute. But it is equally clear that the time has come for a penetrating examination of the system's future and, perhaps, some radical surgery on its parts.

Selected Bibliography

Books

Ball, Robert M., *Social Security Today and Tomorrow,* Columbia University Press, 1978.

Campbell, Colin D., ed., *Financing Social Security,* American Enterprise Institute, 1979.

Campbell, Rita Ricardo, *Social Security: Promise and Reality,* Hoover Institution Press, 1977.

Lubove, Roy, *The Struggle for Social Security, 1900-1935,* Harvard University Press, 1968.

Shore, Warren, *Social Security: The Fraud in Your Future,* MacMillan Publishing Co., 1975.

Articles

Ball, Robert M., "Income Security for the Elderly," *National Journal,* Oct. 28, 1978.

Califano, Joseph A. Jr., "U.S. Policy for the Aging — A Commitment to Ourselves," *National Journal,* Sept. 30, 1978.

Conte, Christopher R., "Financing Squeeze Forces New Assessment of Social Security," *Congressional Quarterly Weekly Report,* March 17, 1979.

Donnelly, Harrison H., "Aging U.S. Population Poses Threat to Retirement Systems," *Congressional Quarterly Weekly Report,* March 17, 1979.

Orshansky, Mollie, "Counting the Poor: Another Look at the Poverty Profile," *Social Security Bulletin,* January 1965.

Platt, Charles M., "Social Security: Will It Be There When You Need It?" *U.S. News & World Report,* April 30, 1979.

Reports and Studies

Campbell, Colin D., "The 1977 Amendments to the Social Security Act," American Enterprise Institute, 1978.

Colberg, Marshall R., "The Social Security Retirement Test: Right or Wrong?" American Enterprise Institute, 1978.

Editorial Research Reports, "Mandatory Retirement," 1977 Vol. II, p. 849; "Pension Problems," 1976 Vol. I, p. 363; "Medicare and Medicaid After Ten Years," 1975 Vol. II, p. 523; "Retirement Security," 1974 Vol. II, p. 965; "Social Security Financing," 1972 Vol. II, p. 705; "Plight of the Aged," 1971 Vol. II, p. 863.

Mitchell, William C., "The Popularity of Social Security," American Enterprise Institute, 1977.

Penner, Rudolph G., "Social Security Financing Proposals," American Enterprise Institute, 1977.

PUBLIC CONFIDENCE AND ENERGY

by

**William Sweet
and Sandra Stencel**

**May 25
1 9 7 9**

Editor's Note: Since this report was originally published in the late spring of 1979, America's oil import picture has been worsened by trouble with the revolutionary government in Iran, which later in the year cut off its petroleum exports to the United States. At the same time, President Carter's ability to rally public opinion for conservation measures apparently was strengthened by U.S. indignation over the Iranians' seizure of American diplomatic personnel as hostages. However, as the year 1979 drew to a close, Congress had not been impelled to approve the major energy legislation Carter sought.

PUBLIC CONFIDENCE AND ENERGY

PUBLIC skepticism about the seriousness of the energy situation has plagued President Carter throughout his administration. When he proposed his "National Energy Plan" to Congress in April 1977 with great fanfare, Carter asked the American people to respond to energy shortages with what he called "the moral equivalent of war." Four months later, a CBS-New York Times poll asked the following question: "President Carter has told us that we are running out of oil and natural gas. Do you think things are as bad as the president said?" Of those responding, only 33 percent said yes while 57 percent said no.

Despite repeated presidential addresses, unceasing media attention and new problems with Middle East oil suppliers, the American public's views on energy have barely changed in the past two years. According to a recent poll taken by NBC News and the Associated Press, over half the people questioned — 54 percent — thought the energy shortage was a hoax.[1] The difficulty of convincing the public that there is an oil supply problem has been conceded by government officials. A Department of Energy official sees the oil supply problem "not like the kind of crisis we had with Pearl Harbor, but more like a cancer. . . ." Another spokesman for the department said that telling people oil inventories are being depleted "doesn't have the clarion call that it's time to hit the trenches."[2]

Pollster Patrick Caddell has said that President Carter never expected to build a strong national consensus in favor of his energy policy. "It is easily demonstrated from surveys...," Caddell wrote last year, "that it would be next to impossible to construct a 'popular' energy policy, since large segments of the public oppose most possible solutions if they 'cost' anything, whether that cost is expressed in taxes, higher prices, or environmental risk. Even advocating policies that have clear majority support — such as nuclear power or offshore drilling — runs the risk of alienating the outspoken of such policies."[3]

---

[1] The poll was conducted on April 30 and May 2 and released on May 3, 1979.
[2] Both officials quoted in the *Congressional Quarterly Weekly Report,* Feb. 10, 1979, pp. 225-226.
[3] Patrick Caddell, "Why Kevin Phillips Misfired: A Reply on Energy," *Public Opinion,* July-August 1978, pp. 55-56.

One problem in convincing Americans of the seriousness of the energy situation is the public's deep-seated faith in American institutions and talents. Many people appear to believe that "Yankee Ingenuity" eventually will solve whatever energy problems the nation faces. A report recently published by the Council on Environmental Quality indicated that some of the public's optimism may be justified. "The technology to increase greatly the productivity of the U.S. energy system is at hand," the report stated. Increased use of today's most advanced technologies "would allow the U.S. economy to operate on 30-40 percent less energy." But the council emphasized that "achieving low energy growth will not be easy or cheap."[4]

Public Perception of Carter Energy Policies

The public's perception of President Carter's handling of energy problems has declined steadily *(see graph p. 145)*. Between February and April of this year the people who believed Carter was doing a good or excellent job on energy dropped from 19 to 14 percent, according to the NBC-AP poll. He and members of his administration have been accused of crying wolf too often, issuing contradictory and misleading statements, and responding to emergencies in a fashion that failed to inspire confidence.

To illustrate the credibility problem, critics point to recent White House statements on gasoline supplies. On April 24, Carter predicted there would be a shortage of gasoline this summer "and an even greater shortage . . . next year." But after a meeting with Gov. Edmund G. (Jerry) Brown Jr. on May 16 to discuss California's gasoline shortage, the president sounded more optimistic. He announced a series of steps to alleviate the problem in California and predicted that after gasoline supplies on the West Coast hit a low point at the end of May they would begin to increase in June.

Secretary of Energy James R. Schlesinger provided an equally optimistic forecast. "We hope the worst is over," he said at a press briefing at the White House on May 16. Schlesinger said oil imports are expected to increase during the summer and that American refiners would have more leeway to draw down existing crude oil stocks, allowing them to produce more gasoline. Because of these factors, he said, it might be possible to increase national gasoline deliveries up to the 1978 level; they are currently running at about 93 percent of that level. But the next day presidential Press Secretary Jody Powell told reporters that he wanted to "inject a note of caution" into the national debate on gasoline supplies. Powell said that even with the improve-

---

[4] Council on Environmental Quality, "The Good News About Energy," U.S. Government Printing Office, 1979.

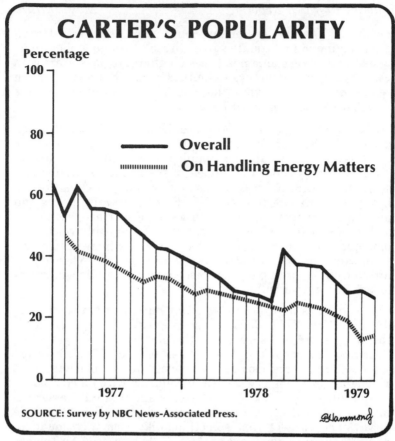

CARTER'S POPULARITY

Percentage

——— Overall

⸺⸺ On Handling Energy Matters

1977   1978   1979

SOURCE: Survey by NBC News-Associated Press.

B.Hammond

ments forecast by Carter and Schlesinger, gasoline supplies will fall about 5 percent short of demand over the summer.

"The White House seems caught between competing objectives in its portrayals of the shortage," *Washington Post* reporter Edward Walsh wrote May 18. "On the one hand, Carter has issued his dire predictions of worsening shortages while attempting to prod Congress into enacting his 'windfall profits' tax on the oil industry and as part of his unsuccessful attempt to win congressional approval of his standby gasoline rationing plan. But when confronted with signs of anger and panic among motorists in parts of the country ... the official predictions, while stressing that the nation's 'fundamental' energy problems remain unchanged, turned more optimistic on the question of short-run gasoline supplies."

White House Response to Energy Emergency

Beginning in California late in April, gasoline shortages similar to those experienced during the Arab oil embargo of 1973-74 *(see p. 149)* reappeared in several parts of the country. Some service stations closed weekends and others restricted the amount of gasoline customers could purchase. Gov. Brown permitted individual counties to institute a rationing plan limiting motorists to gasoline purchases on alternate days. Cars with license plates ending in even numbers could obtain gas only on even-numbered days, while those ending in odd numbers were restricted to odd-numbered days.

Gasoline shortages have been predicted since last fall, when Iranian oil workers first went on strike in the early stage of the revolutionary upheaval that toppled the shah.[5] But despite official warnings about the impact of the Iranian situation and the subsequent decision by other members of the Organization of Petroleum Exporting Countries (OPEC)[6] to raise prices and cut back oil production, the recent gasoline shortages seemed to catch much of the public by surprise. Many people voiced the opinion that the shortage amounted to nothing more than a plot by industry and government to drive up prices. When gas is hard to find, according to their reasoning, the public will grumble less about $1-a-gallon gasoline.

Such remarks have been greeted by outcries from the Carter administration. "The American people refuse to face the inevitable prospect of fuel shortages," the president told a gathering of business leaders at the White House on May 15. He asserted that Americans "are looking for scapegoats" in believing that the federal government has been in collusion with oil companies to bring about the shortages. Carter made a similar assertion during a political visit to California 10 days earlier. "We have known since 1973-74 that something like this was bound to happen," the president said on May 5. "The reason for the gas lines . . . is that we have failed to be prepared."

He had equally harsh words for the House of Representatives, which on May 10 defeated his standby gasoline rationing plan by a 159-246 vote. The president described himself as "shocked" and "embarrassed" by the House action, and he criticized members for letting "political timidity prevent their taking action in the interest of the nation."

The gas rationing plan, which would have been activated only in the case of a shortage far worse than the nation now is experiencing, was passed by the Senate on May 9. It was one of four energy emergency proposals submitted by President Carter to Congress on Feb. 27, 1979 *(see box p. 147)*. Only one of the four — a plan for restricting thermostat settings in non-residential buildings — was approved by Congress.[7] Plans that would have restricted outdoor advertising lighting and given the presi-

---

[5] See "Iran Between East and West," *E.R.R.*, 1979 Vol. I, pp. 65-84.

[6] Algeria, Ecuador, Gabon, Indonesia, Iraq, Kuwait, Libya, Nigeria, Qatar, Saudi Arabia, the United Arab Emirates, and Venezuela.

[7] The House approved the measure on May 10, the Senate on May 2.

Energy Emergency Plans

Congress first asked the executive branch for emergency conservation and rationing plans in 1975 as part of the Energy Policy and Conservation Act. Though the law stated that the plans should be sent to Congress within 180 days, which meant by June 1976, the Ford administration did not present its proposals until January 1977, just before Carter took office. The Carter administration, unhappy with the Ford plan, withdrew it and began to write its own proposal. A preliminary plan was published in the *Federal Register* on June 28, 1978.

Under the 1975 law Congress can only approve or reject the president's emergency conservation and rationing plans. Once the standby plans are enacted, the president can implement them only if there is a "severe energy supply disruption" or if international agreements required a cut in consumption. However, either house of Congress would have 15 days to veto imposition of a gas rationing plan. Once triggered, the plans could remain active for only nine months. To extend them would require a new finding of a severe supply disruption.

dent authority to limit weekend sales of gasoline were defeated, along with the gas rationing proposal.

Credibility Problems; Harrisburg Aftermath

Aside from those who see a plot in gasoline shortages, there are people who say the government has contributed to public confusion. Ever since the Arab embargo, reports of shortages and gluts have alternated with bewildering frequency, and official explanations have done little to clarify the situation. In the immediate aftermath of the embargo, U.S. leaders warned that OPEC was in a position to extort higher prices at will and that continued reliance on Arab oil would expose the country to repeated shortages. But between 1974 and 1978 news of oil gluts far exceeded stories of shortages. During this period there was only one sizable OPEC price boost — a 10 percent increase on Jan. 1, 1977. The oil producers found their power to dictate prices during this period eroding, and only the cut-off of Iranian supplies restored their bargaining position.

Secretary Schlesinger seized on the Iranian crisis to drive home the urgency of the U.S. energy situation. He asserted repeatedly that the Iranian revolution had left the world short two million barrels of oil per day, and that the U.S. shortfall was creeping toward 800,000 barrels. But on April 1, newspapers published reports of a Central Intelligence Agency study indicating that world petroleum production in the first two months of 1979 was up by nearly three million barrels per day over the same period of 1978. A soon-to-be-released Congressional Research Service study is said to place the U.S. shortfall at just 80,000 barrels rather than 800,000.

147

Until the morning California motorists started to line up by the hundreds at filling stations, most talk among Washington energy officials had been of measures to relieve a West Coast oil glut. The unexpected shortage has since been explained largely in terms of panic buying by drivers; a misallocation of oil by the energy companies; an exceptionally sharp rise in California's demand for oil during January and February; increased production of home heating oil rather than gasoline; and a mismatch between the kinds of oil produced in Alaska and the kinds needed in California.

The accident at the Three Mile Island nuclear power plant near Harrisburg, Pa., on March 28 delivered a series of damaging blows to the credibility of energy officials and policy makers. After more than two days of mildly reassuring statements from the government, it was announced that an explosive hydrogen bubble had formed in the reactor. Worse yet, Nuclear Regulatory Commission (NRC) officials made it clear that they might not be able to get rid of the bubble without losing control of the reactor. As it turned out, they eliminated the bubble with unexpected ease.

It so happened that transcripts of the NRC's deliberations during the crisis were released at the behest of Rep. Morris K. Udall, D-Ariz., chairman of the House Interior Committee, and these seemed to show that officials had spent about as much time worrying about public relations as about how to deal with the emergency at hand. At one critical moment during the emergency NRC Chairman Joseph M. Hendrie confessed that he and his colleagues were "operating almost entirely in the blind."

Schlesinger, Energy Dept. Under Criticism

The NRC's parent organization, the Department of Energy (DOE), itself has become "a model of confusion — a superagency finding it hard to awaken from the bureaucratic stupor it inherited." Such sharp criticism — this by an environmental writer[8] — is widespread in Washington. The department, *The Wall Street Journal* suggested last year, should change its name to DONE — the Department of No Energy. "Clearly the true function of that labyrinthine, super-expensive department is to prevent Americans from having energy," the paper commented further.[9] John Osborne wrote in *The New Republic* that it is hard to escape "an overwhelming impression that the Department of Energy under Secretary Schlesinger is a godawful policy and administrative mess."[10] DOE, so the litany

---

[8] Janet Marinelli, "Energy Shortage at DOE," *Environmental Action*, Nov. 4, 1978, p. 12.
[9] *The Wall Street Journal*, Aug. 7, 1978.
[10] *The New Republic*, March 31, 1979.

of charges goes, is fragmented in warring fiefdoms, each committed to pet projects pursued for decades before the department came into existence in 1977.

Defenders of the department concede that it has had start-up problems but stress the difficulties inherent in organizing a mammoth new organization at a time of crisis. DOE Public Affairs Director Jim Bishop contends that the "tennis show phenomenon" — department officials trotting up to the Capitol on their own to fight for cherished programs — is being brought under control. Bishop adds that detractors should remind themselves that the department happens to be dealing with "the most fractious political issue in the country today."[11]

Worsening U.S. Energy Situation

THE CAMPAIGN to convince the public of the seriousness of the U.S. energy situation has been waged unceasingly since the Arab oil embargo of 1973-74. The embargo was imposed Oct. 18, 1973, by Saudi Arabia and then other Arab members of OPEC displeased with America's pro-Israeli policy during the October Middle East war. It remained in effect until March 18, 1974.[12]

The most visible effects of the embargo were the long lines at service stations. In addition, most service stations closed on Sundays, sharply curtailing weekend driving and leaving many motels and ski resorts empty. Fear of running out of heating oil led office managers and homeowners to turn down thermostats and many Americans donned sweaters indoors during the 1973-74 winter. But the more fundamental effect of the embargo was a fourfold increase in the cost of foreign oil. From Oct. 1, 1973, to Jan. 1, 1974, the average price of a barrel of oil imported into the United States rose from $3.00 to $11.65.

Fuel was no longer a bargain, as it had been for the entire post-World War II era. Consumer prices soon reflected this leap in the cost of imported oil. Regular gasoline that cost 35 cents a gallon in mid-1973 sold for 56 cents a gallon by August 1974. Along with the price of oil, the price of coal, natural gas, electricity and even firewood increased. The economic impact was severe. Industrial output dropped; unemployment rose. Sec-

---

[11] Interview, April 11, 1979.

[12] The embargo was also applied to the Netherlands, effectively cutting off oil for most of Western Europe. See "Middle East Reappraisal," *E.R.R.*, 1973 Vol. II, pp. 947-966, and "Arab Oil Money," *E.R.R.*, 1974 Vol. I, pp. 363-382.

retary of State Henry A. Kissinger said that the embargo "cost the United States 500,000 jobs, more than $10 billion in national production and a rampant inflation."[13]

The embargo did not create the energy crisis. It simply brought dramatically to world attention a fact that experts had been pointing out for some time: The United States was each year consuming more oil and producing less, therefore becoming ever more dependent on imported oil. As succeeding administrations tried to educate the public on this fact, they employed similar weapons and confronted similar problems.

Nixon-Ford Push for Project Independence

Two weeks after the imposition of the Arab oil embargo, on Nov. 7, 1973, President Nixon delivered a televised address to the nation. The United States was "heading toward the most acute shortages of energy since World War II," Nixon warned. His response: Project Independence, a plan to make the United States self-sufficient in energy by 1980. In trying to rally support for Project Independence, Nixon employed a level of rhetoric that would characterize much of the debate on energy policy.

"Let us unite in committing the resources of this nation to a major new endeavor, an endeavor that in this bicentennial era we can appropriately call 'Project Independence,' " the president said. "Let us set as our national goal, in the spirit of Apollo, with the determination of the Manhattan Project, that by the end of this decade we will have developed the potential to meet our own energy needs without depending on any foreign energy sources. . . . We have an energy crisis, but there is no crisis of the American spirit."

Energy experts quickly described the goal of energy self-sufficiency by 1980 as unrealistic, and by 1974 the goal was quietly redefined as independence from insecure foreign sources of oil. The timetable also was quietly shifted back five years, to 1985. Soon after taking office President Ford said that "no nation has or can have within its borders everything necessary for a full and rich life for all its people. Independence cannot mean isolation. The aim of Project Independence is not to set the United States apart from the rest of the world; it is to enable the United States to do its part more effectively in the world's effort to provide more energy."

Early in 1974 the Arab oil embargo was lifted. As the memory of the long gasoline lines faded, the problem of energy began to recede from national attention. A Gallup Poll released on Jan.

---

[13] Quoted in Congressional Quarterly's *Congress and the Nation,* Vol. IV (1977), p. 201.

31, 1974 indicated that the energy crisis was the most important problem facing the nation. Within six months energy had slipped to fourth on the list, behind the high cost of living, dissatisfaction with government and Watergate.

President Ford in January 1975 offered a plan to cut energy consumption and stimulate domestic energy production by relying on higher fuel prices. Prices would have been allowed to rise through a combination of import fees and a lifting of federal controls. Sensitized by rising unemployment and seemingly uncontrollable inflation, Democratic leaders were wary of any plan to raise prices or cut back energy use, fearing such moves would further slow the already sluggish economy. They instead advocated a tax-based approach that involved increasing gasoline taxes to encourage conservation and providing tax incentives to spur energy production.

Congress rejected both the Ford and Democratic leadership approaches, coming up instead with the more moderate "Energy Policy and Conservation Act." Its most controversial provision required the president to continue federal controls on the price of domestic oil into early 1979.[14] Congressional leaders of both parties ended 1975 with a sense of frustration and weariness born of the long wrangle over energy. "What began as a thrilling and dramatic enterprise has degenerated at times into a farcical comedy of frustrations," said Rep. Jim Wright, D-Texas. "Too often Congress has been simply unwilling to make the hard decisions and take the difficult steps necessary to achieve energy sufficiency for the United States." A year later, Wright was even more critical of Congress's record on energy: "Since the Arab oil embargo three years ago, we have tried to do a few timid things to reduce consumption, but they have not been very successful."

Reaction to Carter's 1977 Energy Proposal

During the 1976 presidential campaign, Carter emphasized the need for conservation as the foundation of the nation's effort to move into a stronger energy posture. Critical of the failure of the nation's leaders to convince the American people of the urgency of the energy problem, he promised to institute a comprehensive conservation program to cut back on energy waste. "Americans are willing to make sacrifices," he said, "if they understand the reason for them and if they believe the sacrifices are fairly distributed."

The need for a comprehensive energy program was underscored during the winter of 1977-78. A severe cold spell in the

---

[14] President Nixon imposed price controls on domestic oil in 1971, under authority granted him by the Economic Stabilization Act. In 1973, Congress shifted authority for these controls from the original act, which expired in 1974, to the Emergency Petroleum Allocation Act. Authority for the controls was extended in 1974 to Aug. 31, 1975.

East and Midwest caused such rapid depletion of the nation's declining natural gas supplies that many schools and factories were closed and workers went jobless. The day after he took office, President Carter ordered White House thermostats dialed down to a chilly 65 degrees and asked all Americans to follow his example. On Jan. 30, after a trip to hard-hit Pittsburgh, he emphasized that "we are all in it together. Every household that keeps its temperatures too high or wastes fuel contributes to the unemployment of the American people and a damage to our society."

By Feb. 1, 11 states were in emergency status with industries and schools closed by gas cutoffs. Hardest hit by the gas shortages, according to the Federal Power Commission, were Ohio, Pennsylvania, New York, Indiana, Maryland, Idaho and Illinois. Agency estimates were that 8,900 plants closed in the Midwest and East, with 549,000 workers temporarily laid off. Many automobile and steelmakers were unable to reopen before April, the end of the heating season.[15]

Despite the hardships caused by the natural gas shortages, neither the public nor Congress appeared ready to face up to America's growing dependence on foreign energy supplies. This was clear from the reaction to President Carter's energy plan, announced in April 1977. The Carter plan would have empowered the federal government (1) to require industries to make products meeting mandated standards of energy efficiency, (2) to tell businesses to burn certain fuels but not others, (3) to sponsor massive programs encouraging property owners to insulate their buildings, (4) to levy stiff taxes against cars that guzzled too much gasoline, against businesses that burned oil or natural gas and against purchasers of domestically produced oil. The taxes were designed to raise the price of oil so high that consumers would cut back their use of it.

By his own admission, Carter did not expect his program to be popular. A Gallup Poll in April indicated that a majority of Americans thought the energy crisis was something less than "very serious." On April 18, Carter delivered what he termed "an unpleasant talk" to the nation via television in an effort to change America's mind. A White House aide was quoted as calling this speech Carter's "the-sky-is-falling" message.

"With the exception of preventing war, this is the greatest challenge our country will face during our lifetime," Carter said. "The energy crisis has not yet overwhelmed us, but it will if we do not act quickly. . . ." The president recited the facts that he said lay behind the problem. "The oil and natural gas we rely on

---

[15] For background on the 1977 gas supply problem, see Congressional Quarterly's *1977 CQ Almanac*, p. 648.

for 75 percent of our energy are running out.... Domestic production has been dropping steadily at about 6 percent a year. Imports have doubled in the last five years. Our nation's independence ... is becoming increasingly constrained...."

Carter and the Democratic congressional leaders pushed hard to complete action on his energy plan by the end of the year. Carter spoke to the nation via evening television addresses only three times during his first year in Washington; each time the subject was energy. The only speech Carter made to a joint session of Congress during his first year was also on his energy program. When the going got tough on Capitol Hill, the president sent his Cabinet members across the country to plug for the energy plan. Though his critics at time faulted Carter's tactics, it was clear that no other single domestic issue received so much presidential attention in 1977. And yet, the Carter energy plan did not make it through Congress.

There was no single, simple answer why the president's plan failed to clear Congress.[16] But there were a number of clearly identifiable contributing factors, including lack of widespread public support. Gallup Polls throughout the year demonstrated one of the biggest obstacles Carter faced: About half of the nation refused to take the energy crisis very seriously. In mid-December, Gallup reported that 40 percent of those questioned believed that the U.S. energy situation was "very serious"; 42 percent viewed it as "fairly serious"; 15 percent saw the problem as "not at all serious." Those figures had remained virtually unchanged since early April, before the president's plan was presented. "Approximately half of the public can be said to be relatively unconcerned about our energy problems," George Gallup wrote in late June.

Growing Public Distrust of Oil Companies

The absence of a strong body of public opinion behind Carter's program made it difficult to repel a sophisticated lobbying campaign against the plan. On Oct. 13, 1977, the president told a televised news conference that oil company lobbying was transforming his energy package into "the biggest rip-off in history." He said the issue before Congress was "whether the money should be given partially to the oil companies to encourage production and partially to the American people in a fair way or whether it should all be grabbed by the oil companies at the expense of the American consumer."

Carter's attacks on oil industry "rip-offs" fueled the public's growing suspicion of the industry. Between 1967 and 1977

---

[16] Carter's energy plan passed the House virtually intact Aug. 5, but then bogged down in the Senate. For background, see Congressional Quarterly's *1977 CQ Almanac,* pp. 708-745.

Americans who claimed to have "a favorable impression" of the oil industry dropped by 40 points, according to the Opinion Research Organization. The auto industry, in contrast, lost 30 points during the same period.[17]

The oil industry reported record profits for 1973, up an average of 48 percent over 1972. Sen. Henry M. Jackson, D-Wash., termed such profit levels "obscene," a characterization not modified when profits continued to rise with prices. Profits for the first six months of 1974 were up 82 percent over the first six months of 1973. Shyam Sunder, an accounting professor at the University of Chicago, described the record profits as a public relations disaster for the companies. "To many critics of the oil industry little further proof was needed that the oil industry was out to loot the consumer and was being extraordinarily successful," Sunder wrote in 1977.[18] He concluded that the situation in 1973 and 1974 was most likely temporary but the political damage had already been done. A Gallup Poll conducted shortly after the companies began announcing their profits indicated that more Americans blamed the oil companies for the energy crisis than blamed the Arab states that imposed the embargo.

Senator Jackson, as chairman of the Senate Permanent Investigations Subcommittee, held hearings in early 1974 into charges that the fuel shortage had been contrived and that the oil industry's profits were excessive. The companies heatedly denied the charges and some of them resorted to full-page newspaper ads to make their views better known. But public opinion appeared to remain hostile. It was in this atmosphere that Congress early in 1975 moved to revoke the tax depletion allowance for major oil and gas producers, retaining it only for small producers. This tax advantage, enjoyed since 1926, allowed them to reduce the amount of their income subject to federal taxes by a percentage intended to represent the extent to which their oil and gas wells had been depleted through production in that year.

But a direct attack on the structure of the industry — which critics charged was concentrated in too few hands — was beaten back later in 1975 when the Senate refused to require energy companies to divest themselves of all but one aspect of the business — production, transportation, refining or marketing. The narrowness of the margin of defeat, nine votes, was a surprise to both sides, encouraging advocates of divestiture proposals to redouble their efforts and setting off a massive anti-

---

[17] See Seymour Martin Lipset and William Schneider, "How's Business? What the Public Thinks," *Public Opinion,* July-August 1978, p. 44.

[18] Shyam Sunder, *Oil Industry Profits* (1977), p. 66.

divestiture public relations campaign by the industry. In 1976 a divestiture measure was reported to the Senate by the Senate Judiciary Committee, but the leadership did not want to wrestle with the tricky issue in an election year. The bill went no farther and died with adjournment.[19]

Recent Department of Energy allegations that seven major oil companies illegally overcharged their customers by $1.7 billion over the past six years helped revive the animosity that many people feel toward the oil companies.[20] The civil complaints, filed May 1, 1979, charged the companies with improperly shifting lower-priced oil into higher-priced categories, so that customers sometimes paid twice as much as they should have. The charges brought to $3.5 billion the total of pricing violations alleged by the Department of Energy against the oil industry since a special office to audit refiners was established within the agency. The oil companies have denied the charge.

The Department of Energy's allegations came as a number of the nation's largest oil companies reported sharply higher first quarter profits resulting largely from higher world petroleum prices. Exxon, the nation's biggest oil company, said its first quarter profits rose 37 percent over last year. Mobil, the second largest company, and Texaco, the third biggest, each reported an 81 percent increase. Other major oil companies also reported higher profits. The profit figures are not likely to help the oil industry's image problem. Asked who they thought was responsible for the recent increases in the price of gasoline and heating oil, 39 percent of those responding to the recent NBC-AP poll said the oil companies. Only 29 percent blamed the oil producing countries.

Efforts to Win Public Trust

PERHAPS in response to the public's growing mistrust of official rhetoric, President Carter at times this year appeared to adopt a lower profile on energy. In his State of the Union message to Congress, Jan. 23, Carter mentioned energy only once, not even giving it a full sentence. He called on the nation to "...conserve energy, increase production, and speed

---

[19] See "Oil Antitrust Action," *E.R.R.*, 1978 Vol. I, pp. 101-120.

[20] The companies cited and the amount of the alleged overcharges were: Texaco, Inc., $888.3 million; Gulf Oil Co., $578 million; Standard Oil of California, $101.6 million; Atlantic Richfield Co., $42 million; Marathon Oil, $29.1 million; Standard Oil of Indiana, $24.1 million; and Standard Oil of Ohio, $1.7 million.

development of solar power. . . ." His statement was a marked contrast to his 1978 State of the Union address in which he proclaimed: "Never again should we neglect growing crises like the shortage of energy, where further delay will only lead to more harsh and painful solutions."

But a low-key approach often turns out to be hard to sustain. As public concern over recent gasoline shortages intensified and as his energy proposals bogged down in Congress, President Carter seemed to revert with increasing frequency to the rhetoric that marked earlier presidential statements on energy. In a nationally televised speech April 5, Carter warned: "Our national strength is dangerously dependent on a thin line of oil tankers stretching halfway around the earth. . . ." He called on Americans to drive less and support other conservation efforts. The nation's energy problem "is serious — and it's getting worse," Carter said. "There is no single answer. We must produce more. We must conserve more. . . . Each one of us will have to use less oil and pay more for it."

Carter has used particularly strong language in urging Congress to pass his windfall profits tax on the nation's oil companies *(see box, p. 157)*. "Every vote against [the tax] will be a vote for excessive oil company profits and for reliance on the whims of the foreign oil cartel," Carter said in his April 5 address. "As surely as the sun will rise," he continued, the oil industry will "fight to keep the profits which they have not earned. Unless you speak out, they will have more influence on Congress than you do." The president continued his verbal assault on oil producers at an Oval Office ceremony April 26, when he announced the details of his plan to tax oil company profits. He described the oil companies as "already awash with their greatest profits" since the 1973 oil embargo.

Carter's recent statements on nuclear power hark back to his campaign promise to de-emphasize atomic energy. Just last year the president was promoting a bill to expedite the licensing of nuclear power plants. But during a meeting with the organizers of a May 6 anti-nuclear demonstration in Washington, Carter said his administration wanted "to shift toward alternate energy supplies and also strict conservation programs to minimize the requirement for the use of nuclear power."

In the wake of the Three Mile Island accident, there has been a sharp drop in support for nuclear power. Over 40 percent of those reponding to a poll conducted by *The New York Times* and CBS News in early April opposed construction of new nuclear power plants, compared to 21 percent two years earlier. Two-thirds of those responding to a Gallup Poll in April said that nuclear power plant operations should be reduced until

Decontrol and the 'Windfall Profits' Tax

In a nationally televised speech April 5, President Carter announced a gradual end to controls on domestic oil prices. Decontrol would be phased in, starting June 1 when existing mandatory price controls may be lifted at the president's discretion — unless Congress rejects his plan. The president's authority is provided by the Energy Policy and Conservation Act of 1975 *(see p. 151)*. That law expires Sept. 30, 1981, ending all controls then. The White House expects higher prices resulting from decontrols will provide the petroleum industry the incentive to increase production 330,000 barrels a day and as much as 800,000 barrels a day in 1985.

To prevent U.S. oil companies from reaping "huge and undeserved profits" as a result of decontrols, Carter asked Congress to enact a "windfall profits" tax. Stuart Eizenstat, the White House domestic policy chief, predicted April 26 that lifting price controls would produce $15.4 billion through 1981 in increased income for domestic oil producers. Of that, $3.3 billion — about 21 percent — would be collected as windfall profits taxes, he said. About $5.2 billion would go to the federal government as income taxes and the states would collect $1 billion in taxes. Oil companies would keep the remaining $6 billion of the original $15.4 billion. The windfall profits tax revenues would go into an Energy Security Trust Fund to help low income families deal with higher energy costs, improve mass transit and reduce U.S. dependence on foreign oil.

Congressional critics of decontrol say it would hurt consumers and provide no assurance it would increase domestic oil production. In the Senate, the fight to extend price controls is being led by Edward M. Kennedy, D-Mass., and Henry M. Jackson, D-Wash., chairman of the Energy and Natural Resources Committee. The leading proponent of controls in the House is Toby Moffett, D-Conn. The position of those favoring extension of controls was strengthened recently when House Democrats indicated their opposition to the administration's decontrol plan.

stricter safety regulations were put into effect. Only 40 percent had taken this position in 1976.

Support for Expanded Energy Production

In a 1978 article in *Public Opinion* magazine, conservative author Kevin P. Phillips wrote that one reason Carter's 1977 energy plan did not win widespread public or congressional support was that "the White House miscalculated the degree of public willingness to rest the economic future of the United States more on energy conservation than on expanded energy production." [21] Phillips backed his statement with the results of several polls. For example, a Gallup Poll published in late April

---

[21] Kevin P. Phillips, "The Energy Battle: Why the White House Misfired," *Public Opinion,* May-June 1978, p. 10.

Public's Response to Energy Shortages

Turned down thermostat	44%
Reduced driving	33
Turning off lights	27
Conserve electricity (generally)	15
Insulated home	12
Cut down on use of appliances	10
Use wood as fuel	7
Bought gas-saving car, motorcycle	5
Car pool	3
Use less hot water	2
Reduce water consumption	2
Minimum use of air-conditioner	2
Nothing	15

Total adds up to more than 100 percent due to multiple responses.

Source: The Gallup Poll, March 25, 1979.

1977 asked the following question: "Some people think the Carter [energy] plan puts too much emphasis on conservation of energy and not enough on the development of new energy sources. Do you agree or disagree with this opinion?" Gallup found that 59 percent of the respondents agreed, while only 30 percent disagreed.

The president's energy proposals still place great emphasis on conservation, but in his April 5 television address Carter asked Americans to "join together in a great national effort to use American technology to give us energy security in the years ahead."One of the measures Carter proposed to lessen U.S.

reliance on foreign energy supplies was "more rapid development and use of solar power." Over half of those reponding to the recent NBC-AP poll said that solar energy will be the best source of power in 20 years.

But the same poll indicated that few people are willing to spend much more money to assure solar development. Nearly a quarter of those reponding (24 percent) said they would not be willing to pay more "to replace our current sources of energy with solar and other renewable sources." Only 26 percent were willing to pay over $10 more a month to assure development of new energy sources.

Public, Government Conservation Efforts

Despite continued skepticism about the authenticity of the energy crisis, many Americans already have adjusted to a more energy-conscious lifestyle. Only 15 percent of those who answered questions in a Gallup Poll on March 25 said they were not doing anything to cut their energy consumption *(see box, p. 158)*. Some 70 percent of those in an earlier Gallup survey favored retaining the 55-mile-per-hour speed limit, the law adopted in 1974 because of fuel shortages. Half of the people questioned in the recent NBC-AP Poll said they had cut back their driving by 15 miles a week in the month before the survey was taken.

Americans also are driving more fuel-efficient cars. Detroit had expected small cars to account for about 47 percent of all sales of American-made cars this year. The actual share, as of April 1979, was 54 percent. Imports, mostly small and gas thrifty, now account for more than 22 percent of all sales, a record share. At the same time, sales of gas-guzzling cars and recreation vehicles are down sharply. "The big-car industry is going down like a rock," Chrysler President Lee Iacocca said recently.[22]

According to a report released by the congressional Office of Technology Assessment (OTA) on April 9, Americans have been cutting down on home energy use by changing their habits and making their homes more energy efficient. The report stated that "the growth in residential energy use in the 1970s has been cut in half from 1960's levels, already saving the equivalent of nearly 2.8 billion barrels of oil since 1970 — nearly equal to all oil produced in the United States in 1978." OTA Acting Director Daniel De Simone noted that "residential energy conservation is an instance of acting in one's own self-interest — saving money on heating and cooling bills — while at the same time serving the public interest by reducing the demand for oil and gas."

[22] Quoted in *Time*, May 21, 1979, p. 15.

The federal government also has taken steps to curb energy consumption. Thermostats in federal buildings have been turned down in winter and up in summer as a conservation measure. In his April 5 energy address President Carter announced that executive-branch employees would lose their free and low-priced parking spaces, starting in October. At present, government-controlled spaces rent for as little as $5 or $6 a month. The Carter directive would raise the rentals in stages to levels comparable to those charged by commercial parking facilities in the national capital area. In some areas of downtown Washington, monthly parking rates run as high as $60 or $70.

Many federal agencies continue to maintain fleets of cars, vans and buses for transporting employees to other agencies for short assignments or visits and then back again. Many of these trips would be made just as easily, and in some cases more quickly, on Washington's subway system. The federal government has some distance to go before it can persuade the public that it is doing as much to save energy as it expects the rest of the country to do.

Selected Bibliography
Books

George H. Gallup, *The Gallup Poll: Public Opinion, 1972-1977*, Scholarly Resources, 1978.
Leon N. Lindberg, ed., *The Energy Syndrome*, Lexington Books, 1977.
Dorothy K. Newman and Dawn Day, *The American Energy Consumer*, Ballinger, 1975.

Articles

Donald F. Anthrop, "The Carter Energy Plan and the American West," *The Bulletin of the Atomic Scientists*, January 1978.
Patrick H. Caddell, "Why Kevin Phillips Misfired," *Public Opinion.*, July-August 1978.
Seymour Martin Lipset and William Schneider, "How's Business? What the Public Thinks," *Public Opinion*, July-August 1978.
Janet Marinelli, "Energy Shortage at DOE," *Environmental Action*, November 4, 1978.
"Motivating the Troops for War," *Psychology Today*, April 1979.
Kevin P. Phillips, "The Energy Battle: Why the White House Misfired," *Public Opinion*, May-June 1978.
Eugene Rosa, "The Public and the Energy Problem," *The Bulletin of the Atomic Scientists*, April 1978.

Reports and Studies

A Time to Choose: America's Energy Future, final report of the Ford Foundation's Energy Policy Project, Ballinger, 1974.
Editorial Research Reports, "Oil Imports," 1978 Vol. II, p. 621; "America's Coal Economy," 1978 Vol. I, p. 281; "Oil Antitrust Action," 1978 Vol. I, p. 101; "Natural Gas Shortage," 1975 Vol. II, p. 805; "Future of Utilities," 1975 Vol. I, p. 185.

AFFIRMATIVE ACTION UNDER ATTACK

by

**Kennedy P. Maize
and Sandra Stencel**

**Mar. 30
1 9 7 9**

Editor's Note: The Weber challenge to affirmative action, a case prominently mentioned in this Report, was turned back by the Supreme Court on June 27, 1979. By a 5 to 2 vote, the court ruled that employers and unions could establish voluntary programs, including the use of quotas, to aid minorities and women in employment. Such programs were legal, the court said, even when there was no evidence of past discrimination by the employers.

A suit by Sears, Roebuck & Co., mentioned prominently on the following pages, was dismissed on May 15, 1979, in U.S. District Court in Washington, D.C. Judge June L. Green said the company's allegation of conflicting U.S. rules and policies in regard to employment was "not sufficiently concrete" to give the company legal standing to have its case tried on its merits in federal court.

AFFIRMATIVE ACTION
UNDER ATTACK

IN THE PAST 15 years, the United States has made progress toward eliminating discrimination in employment. Under pressure from the federal government to take "affirmative action" to prevent racial or sexual discrimination, many of the nation's businesses have made a concerted effort to hire and promote blacks, members of other minority groups and women. Complying with the government's anti-discrimination rules, however, frequently is time-consuming, complex and frustrating. Many employers complain that they are trapped between the government's demands to increase opportunities for women and minorities on the one hand, and, on the other, charges by white males that affirmative action constitutes reverse discrimination.[1]

The Supreme Court on March 28 heard oral arguments in the case of Brian F. Weber, a Louisiana man who charged that a special program aimed at moving blacks and women into better jobs made him a victim of reverse discrimination. Weber was refused admission to an in-plant craft-training program at a plant operated by the Kaiser Aluminum and Chemical Corp. in Gramercy, La. He was turned down because half of the slots in the program were set aside for blacks and women. This affirmative action "set aside" in the training program had been agreed upon by Kaiser and the United Steelworkers union as part of a voluntary effort to increase minority participation in skilled jobs in the aluminum industry.

Weber went to federal court, contesting his rejection as reverse discrimination. He won in both federal district court and in a U.S. court of appeals (for the fifth circuit, New Orleans). The Steelworkers, the company and the Justice Department all asked the Supreme Court to review the appeals court's decision, and last December it agreed to do so.

The Justice Department, in its petition to the Supreme Court, suggested the case be sent back to the appeals court for reconsideration in light of the *Bakke* decision. The Supreme Court, on June 28, 1978, had ruled in favor of Alan Bakke, the white engineer who charged that reverse discrimination had blocked his efforts to enroll in the medical school at the University of California at Davis. The court said that universities may

---

[1] See "Reverse Discrimination," *E.R.R.*, 1976 Vol. II, pp. 561-580.

not set aside a quota of seats in each class for minority group representatives and thus deny white applicants the opportunity to compete for those places. But the court held in the same case that it is constitutionally permissible for schools to consider race as one of the factors that determine which applicants are accepted.[2]

The key question left unresolved in the *Bakke* case — which might be answered by the *Weber* decision — is whether it is permissible for employers and other institutions that have not been found guilty of prior illegal discrimination voluntarily to adopt affirmative action programs, which by their very nature involve some discrimination against majority group members.

In *Bakke,* a five-man majority agreed that some affirmative action programs were permissible under the Constitution's guarantee of equal protection. But the crucial fifth vote, cast by Justice Lewis F. Powell Jr., seemed to be qualified by his view that such programs were permissible only in situations where there had been a clear finding of prior discrimination. In Weber's case, the court of appeals emphasized — in holding the Kaiser training program illegal — that there had been no showing of prior discrimination by Kaiser.

The Justice Department and the Equal Employment Opportunity Commission have argued that this interpretation puts employers in an impossible situation. If they tried to improve the status of minority workers without admitting past errors, they would be open to lawsuits from disgruntled whites; if they admitted that they had discriminated in the past, they would invite damage suits from minority workers. "If permitted to stand," the Solicitor General's office told the Supreme Court, the Weber decision "can be expected to chill voluntary affirmative action programs . . . throughout the country."

The affirmative action program at issue in the Weber case was part of a nationwide agreement reached in 1974 between Kaiser Aluminum and the United Steelworkers. The agreement called for the creation of special training programs at 15 Kaiser plants. The programs would be open to blacks and whites on a 50-50 basis until the minority representation in the skilled jobs was equivalent to minority representation in the work force from which the plant recruited.

In the case of Kaiser's Gramercy plant, located on the Mississippi River halfway between New Orleans and Baton Rouge, blacks made up 39 percent of the area's labor force, but only 15 percent of the plant's employees. Only five out of 290 skilled jobs were filled by blacks. Under the affirmative action pro-

---

[2] See "Burger Court's Tenth Year," *E.R.R.*, 1978 Vol. II, pp. 681-670.

gram, 13 training positions were created and filled with seven blacks and six whites. But after the courts' rulings in the Weber case, Kaiser revised its training programs so as to make no racial differentiation in selecting applicants. Trainees now are selected solely on the basis of seniority. As a result, there was only one black in a recent training class and half a dozen whites.[3]

Sears Suit Calling Federal Rules Unfair

In recent years corporations as well as individuals have begun to resist government efforts to enforce anti-discrimination laws. For example, Harris Trust and Savings Bank of Chicago disagreed with government findings of discrimination by the bank against women and blacks and has gone to court to try to prove that its employment record is fair. The John Hancock Mutual Life Insurance Co. of Boston, ordered by the government in October 1977 to turn over personnel records for examination for possible job discrimination, has so far refused to do so.

Sears, Roebuck & Co., the nation's tenth largest corporation, recently took corporate complaints against government anti-bias rules one step further. In a class-action suit, filed Jan. 24 in U.S. District Court in Washington, D.C., Sears said the government's equal employment opportunity rules and policies were confusing and conflicting, and that companies could not comply with all the guidelines. The company charged that the government itself, not private industry, was responsible for creating an "unbalanced civilian work force" dominated by white males.

The suit, filed on behalf of all general merchandise retailers employing over 15 workers,[4] asked for an injunction requiring the government to issue uniform guidelines to instruct employers how to resolve existing conflicts between affirmative action requirements based on race and sex and those based on veterans status, age, and physical or mental handicap. "It is time to end government policies and practices which are working at cross-purposes, hampering real progress and discouraging voluntary efforts," Sears Chairman Edward R. Telling said Jan. 24 at a press conference in Chicago, the company's headquarters.

In theory, a victory for Sears could halt nearly all enforcement of equal employment opportunity laws. The Equal Employment Opportunity Commission, one of 10 government agencies named as defendants in the suit,[5] called the lawsuit an attempt by

---

[3] See Steven V. Roberts, "The Bakke Case Moves to the Factory," *The New York Times Magazine,* Feb. 25, 1979, p. 37.

[4] The federal government has job-discrimination jurisdiction only over businesses with 15 or more employees.

[5] The others are the Department of Labor and its Office of Federal Contract Compliance; the Department of Commerce and its Bureau of the Census and Office of Federal Statistical Policy and Standards; the Department of Justice; the Department of Health, Education and Welfare; the Department of Housing and Urban Development; and the Federal Agency Council on the 1980 Census.

Sears to offset discrimination charges pending against the company. The EEOC has been investigating Sears' employment practices since 1973. Negotiations between the commission and Sears broke down last January, reportedly after Sears objected to government contentions that it should give back pay to employees previously discriminated against and to government demands that the company establish mandatory hiring goals. The EEOC now is planning to take the company to court.

The commission is prohibited by law from disclosing its charges against Sears until it actually files suit. But on Feb. 25, *The Washington Post* reported that it had obtained a copy of a 1977 EEOC decision that described "patterns of sex, race and national origin discrimination at all levels" of the company. The decision asserted that "nearly 100 percent of major personnel decisions" at Sears "are made by a network of Anglo male supervisors without the benefit of objective standards." The commission charged that Sears was "restricting blacks and Spanish-surnamed Americans to lower-paying, less desirable jobs;" "failing to hire blacks and/or Spanish-surnamed Americans" for jobs in certain stores "in proportion to their rate of application;" relegating women to lower-paying, less-desirable jobs, and in some cases paying women less than the men, and blacks less than "Anglos" for the same work.

Sears has called the government allegations unfair because they do not take into account either the progress the company has made in hiring and promoting women and minorities or the effect of federal policies on its work force. In 1977, 19.9 percent of the company's 400,000 employees were minority members, compared with 8.7 percent in 1965. Minorities held 10.5 percent of the management positions in 1977, up from 1.4 percent in 1965. About 36 percent of the company's managers were women in 1977, compared with 20 percent in 1965.

In its suit against the government, Sears said past government policies were responsible for the low numbers of women and minority group members in management in the late 1960s and early 1970s. Until recently, the company charged, men were dominant in the labor force largely because of the GI Bill of Rights, veterans preference laws, restrictions on the number of women and blacks in the armed forces, the types of military assignments available to them, and various male-oriented vocational and educational programs administered by government.

U.S. Agency Revisions to Meet Criticism

The federal government has not been oblivious to the problems confronting companies trying to establish affirmative action programs. Last December the Equal Employment Opportunity Commission announced a new policy to protect employers from charges of reverse discrimination for voluntarily hiring and promoting women and minority members. Under the new plan, the EEOC will not proceed with a reverse discrimination investigation if it is determined that the company's affirmative action program had been undertaken "in good faith" and in accordance with new EEOC guidelines. In addition, in a private lawsuit brought by an employee, such as Brian Weber has done, the company could obtain a ruling from the commission that it had acted in accordance with government guidelines, and use that ruling as a defense in court.

To qualify for the immunity, a company's affirmative action plan must meet the EEOC's definition of "reasonable." Under the new guidelines, which took effect on Jan. 11, 1979, employers are expected to conduct a "self-analysis" of their employment systems. If they discover a "reasonable basis" for concluding that affirmative action is needed, they are expected to initiate a plan "that is reasonable in relation to the problem disclosed." To further encourage employers to set up voluntary affirmative action plans, the EEOC said that the reverse discrimination protection would be extended to companies that did not formally admit they were violating civil rights laws when they initiated their affirmative action programs.

Complaints by U.S. businesses frequently centered on the diffusion of enforcement responsibilities among numerous government agencies, including the EEOC, the Departments of Labor and Justice, the Civil Service Commission and the Equal Employment Opportunity Coordinating Council. This diffusion of responsibilities, they said, resulted in inconsistent standards of compliance, inconsistent paperwork requirements and duplicative investigative efforts. Last year the Carter administration took steps to remedy the situation. Under a reorganization plan, most fair-employment-enforcement programs were consolidated into the EEOC and the Labor Department's Office of Federal Contract Compliance. "The plan will . . . reduce the burden of equal employment enforcement on business by consolidating the agencies involved," Carter said on May 6.[6]

The first portion of the plan, making the EEOC the government's policy-making body on job bias, went into effect on July 1, 1978. Six months later the EEOC assumed responsibility for equal employment opportunity for federal employees from the Civil Service Commission. The plan also calls for the EEOC to take over responsibility from the Labor Department for enforc-

---

[6] Under a separate reorganization plan, approved by Congress in August 1978, the Civil Service Commission was divided into two new agencies — the Office of Personnel Management and the Merit Systems Protection Board. The Reorganization Act of 1977 allows the president to submit to Congress plans for reorganizing federal agencies. The plans take effect unless disapproved by the House or Senate within 60 days.

ing both the Equal Pay Act and the Age Discrimination in Employment Act, as of July 1, 1979. The Office of Federal Contract Compliance was given overall responsibility for enforcing presidential orders barring companies that discriminate in employment from holding federal contracts. Before the new plan was put into effect, 12 separate agencies enforced such orders.

The reorganization plan giving new powers to the Equal Employment Opportunity Commission reflects the administration's thinking about the performance of the agency. The EEOC has had a difficult, highly criticized history. The General Accounting Office, for example, reported in September 1976 that "although the EEOC has had some success in obtaining relief for victims of discrimination in specific instances, it does not appear to have yet made the substantial advances against employment discrimination which will be necessary to make a real difference in the employment status of minorities and women."[7]

Eleanor Holmes Norton, the former human rights commissioner for New York City, who became head of EEOC in 1977, has been widely praised for significant progress. Norton has been credited for introducing competent management to the agency, for reducing its tremendous case backlog and for focusing the agency's enforcement efforts on broad "patterns and practices" of discrimination in particular companies or industries rather than isolated instances. When President Carter appointed Norton to the EEOC in 1977, the backlog of discrimination complaints had reached nearly 130,000. The current backlog stands at about 119,000 cases.

Complaints of Federal Double Standard

U.S. businesses frequently complain that the federal government judges itself by anti-bias rules more lenient than those for private industry. Most civil rights analysts have acknowledged the justice of this complaint. The available evidence suggests that Uncle Sam is every bit as discriminatory an employer as many private businesses. A particularly overt form of discrimination in federal employment is a matter of law. The Veterans Preference Act of 1944 stipulated that veterans should be given special consideration when seeking employment with the federal government. This statute granted veterans extra points on competitive Civil Service examinations *(see p. 177).*

An examination of wage discrepancies between male and female and between white and black employees of the Department of Health, Education and Welfare, conducted in 1977 by

---

[7] See also "The Bias in the Government's Anti-Bias Agency," *Fortune,* December 1976, pp. 138-148, and "The Equal Employment Opportunity Commission and How to Make It Work," *Ms.,* February 1977, p. 62.

economist George J. Borjas, indicated that the agency would flunk the anti-discrimination tests it applied to the nation's colleges and universities.[8] Borjas found that the wage differentials among HEW employees were similar to those found in the economy as a whole. The average annual salary for white males in 1977 was $20,897; for black males, $15,333; for white females, $13,395; and for black females, $11,642.

A report released by the General Accounting Office in February 1978 indicated that there were similar problems in the equal employment opportunity program at the Department of Justice. According to the report, blacks and women in the department were concentrated in low-paying jobs and men and women performing the same work had substantial salary differences. "White males in certain occupations were paid an average of about 10 percent more than females with the same levels of education and seniority, working in approximately the same areas of the country, and with the same status as supervisors or subordinates," the report said.[9] It also found that it took an average of 533 days to process complaints, well over the 180-day limit established by law.

Those who follow federal personnel matters suggest that there is nothing unusual about the findings. According to a federal official with years of experience, no federal agency has a good record on job discrimination. This official suggested that, like their counterparts in private industry, federal managers tend to view equal employment opportunity programs as a nuisance, something imposed upon them from above that makes it harder to accomplish the "real work of the agency."

Another factor in the federal record, according to several observers, is a tendency to put the weakest and least effective people into jobs in equal employment opportunity programs. "Many EEO offices around the government are simply turkey farms," said one government officer. "The people in them are either professional blacks-on-the-make, feminist fanatics, bleeding-heart incompetents, or burned-out cases. There are a lot more people living off EEO programs than are being helped by them."

Congressional Self-Exemption; Davis Suit

If programs to enforce equal opportunity statutes are not functioning well in the executive branch, they do not exist at all in the institution that created the laws, the U.S. Congress. Dubbed "the last plantation" by civil rights activists and some

---

[8] Borjas' findings appeared in a paper, "Discrimination in HEW: Is The Doctor Sick or is the Patient Healthy?" distributed in 1978 by the Center for the Study of the Economy and the State at the University of Chicago.

[9] General Accounting Office, "The Department of Justice Should Improve Its Equal Employment Opportunity Programs," Feb. 23, 1978, p. 19.

of its own employees, Congress routinely has avoided listing itself among the employers who have to obey the laws it has passed to protect American workers from discrimination. This double standard, Common Cause President David Cohen said last year, "is illustrative of why people have trouble respecting Congress and why people are angry with Congress, because it sets itself apart."[10]

Two arguments traditionally have been used in defense of exempting Congress from the standards it has set for other employers. One is the doctrine of separation of powers, which would be violated if an executive branch agency such as the Equal Employment Opportunity Commission were allowed to police congressional job practices. Critics of that argument point out that Congress could delegate authority to a new, independent agency outside the executive branch to enforce civil rights laws on Capitol Hill.

The other argument is that politicians and their employees need a loyal, compatible relationship that goes beyond the traditional labor-management situation; thus, the argument goes, members of Congress must have more freedom in hiring and firing. Critics of the loyalty argument say that it is the same one used by private business in opposing the 1964 Civil Rights Act. They acknowledge that members of Congress do have some special needs in staff hiring but maintain those needs can be met without discriminating against minorities and women.

For women and blacks who work on Capitol Hill, discrimination in pay and promotion are the biggest employment gripes. A report released in 1977 by the House Commission on Administrative Review, under the chairmanship of Rep. David R. Obey, D-Wis., found that blacks with a comparable education earned less than whites in every job category. The commission found twice as many women as men were drawing salaries between $10,000 and $15,000 a year. But at salaries over $35,000, men outnumbered women 15 to 1. In the Senate, a survey conducted by the Capitol Hill Women's Political Caucus indicated that between 1975 and 1977 the number of women in professional jobs had more than doubled, but the salary gap had widened. The median salary for women in 1977 was $12,755 (a 24.3 percent increase from 1975), while for men it was $22,879 (a 29.5 percent increase).

House and Senate employees technically can take discrimination complaints to the Ethics committees in both houses. But many workers are afraid to do so because the committees' procedures for handling ethics complaints — particularly in the House — are too intimidating. In recent years, Capitol Hill

---

[10] Quoted in *CQ Weekly Report,* Feb. 11, 1978, p. 339.

Davis v. Passman

The Supreme Court on Feb. 27 heard oral arguments in the case of Shirley Davis, a former House employee who wants to sue her ex-boss, former Rep. Otto E. Passman, D-La., for sex discrimination. Davis was fired in 1974, when she was being groomed to become Passman's administrative assistant. In his letter firing Davis, Passman wrote: "On account of the unusually heavy work load in my Washington office, and the diversity of the job, I concluded that it was essential that the understudy to my administrative assistant be a man."

The Supreme Court will not address the specific charges of sex discrimination, but will decide whether Davis will have the chance to present her evidence in a lower court. Davis first brought suit against Passman in 1974, charging that he had violated her Fifth Amendment right to due process. Passman's attorneys countered that Davis had no legal protection from discrimination. A U.S. District Court in Louisiana agreed, and dismissed her charges. She appealed, and in January 1977 a three-judge panel of the U.S. Fifth Circuit Court of Appeals in New Orleans reversed the earlier ruling. However, Passman asked the full court to review the case and in 1978 the judges voted 12-2 to dismiss Davis' charges.

The appeals court ruled that Davis had no constititutional right to sue Passman for monetary damages. Its decision also said that because Passman was defeated for re-election in 1976, her other claims — for reinstatement and promotion on her job — could not be considered. The appeals court did not directly address the question of whether an employer could bring a sex discrimination suit against a sitting member of Congress if he or she sought relief other than monetary damages. If the Supreme Court agrees with the appeals court, the merits of the Davis case will not be considered.

employees have been pushing for passage of resolutions to set up formal mechanisms for handling discrimination complaints.

The Senate last year considered a resolution that would have set up a three-step grievance system, beginning with an attempt to resolve complaints by informal arbitration. An appeals board of persons from outside the Senate would have considered unresolved complaints, and any remedy recommended by that board could have been appealed to the Senate Ethics Committee. However, the resolution died in the closing days of the 95th Congress.[11]

Prospects for setting up congressional grievance systems could change if the Supreme Court rules later this year that former House employee Shirley Davis can sue former Rep. Otto E. Passman, D-La., for sex discrimination. A favorable ruling for Davis could encourage members of Congress to set up their own procedures in order to discourage more lawsuits *(see box)*.

[11] See *CQ Weekly Report*, Oct. 14, 1978, pp. 2976-2977.

Four Decades of Federal Action

FEDERAL EFFORTS to promote equal employment opportunities can be traced to a specific day — June 25, 1941. President Roosevelt faced the threat of a Negro march on Washington on July 1 if the government did not act to reduce discrimination in the nation's new defense industries. Roosevelt feared that the black protest might destroy, in the words of biographer James MacGregor Burns, "the image of national unity he was carefully fostering."

So on June 25 the president issued Executive Order 8802 "to implement a national policy of non-discriminatory employment and training," applying to all government agencies and to private companies receiving federal contracts. A Fair Employment Practices Committee was set up to oversee compliance, but without any real policing powers. "The order — which someday would be called a landmark step in the nation's greatest internal struggle — was greeted with mixed feelings by Negro leaders and with subdued interest on the part of the big-city press," Burns wrote in *Roosevelt: The Soldier of Freedom* (1970). "The president granted the committee limited funds, and it was slow to get under way. But it was a beginning."

Government employment of blacks in clerical and professional posts increased markedly. But job barriers in private industry did not yield so readily. Local resistance to FEPC orders, blacks' educational shortcomings and restrictive practices of labor unions buttressed long-standing patterns of discrimination. Eventually, as manpower needs became more acute during World War II, factory gates opened wider for black workers. In its final report in 1946, the Fair Employment Practices Committee reported that during the war "Negroes achieved, for the first time, reasonably full and fair employment in the United States" but that "failing a federal guarantee of equal opportunity," it would take a fully operating economy "to create that tightness in the labor market which will make employers seek Negro workers. . . ."[12]

Employment opportunities for women also increased during the war years. Employers' attitudes toward women remained skeptical, but since women in many cases were the only available labor, they were hired. Black women found jobs in manufacturing for the first time. Previous bans on the employment of married women were discarded; by 1944, married women comprised almost half of the female labor force. The war gave women access to more skilled and higher-paying jobs.

---

[12] See "Negro Employment," *E.R.R.*, 1959 Vol. II, pp. 581-583.

Although the war made rapid changes in women's economic status, it did not make a lasting change or profound difference in the public attitude toward working women, nor did it lead to greater equality between the sexes. Women continued to receive less pay than men, to be denied opportunities for training and advancement and to work in separate job categories. During the war, William Henry Chafe observed, "traditional attitudes toward women's place remained largely unchanged."[13]

Efforts to eliminate discrimination in employment continued after the war. President Truman set up machinery in 1948 to overcome continuing discrimination in federal employment, and in 1951 he established a committee to obtain and enforce non-discrimination clauses in federal procurement contracts. President Eisenhower furthered these efforts by creating the President's Committee on Government Contracts, headed by Vice President Richard M. Nixon, in 1953 and the President's Committee on Government Employment Policy in 1955. These committees established procedures for handling complaints, but they lacked enforcement powers. In 1961 President Kennedy issued an executive order abolishing both of the Eisenhower committees and combining their functions in a single Committee on Equal Employment Opportunity. Under the chairmanship of Vice President Lyndon B. Johnson, the committee stepped up efforts to increase jobs and promotions for blacks in the federal government.[14]

1964 Civil Rights Act; Title 7 and EEOC

A milestone in equal employment opportunity for women and minorities was reached with the passage of the Civil Rights Act of 1964. Title VII of that act prohibited discrimination based on race, religion, sex or national origin in hiring or firing, wages and salaries, promotions or any terms, conditions or privileges of employment. The Equal Employment Opportunity Commission was created to administer the act. Initially, the powers of the EEOC were limited largely to investigation and conciliation, but Congress amended the act in 1972 to let the agency go directly to court to enforce the law.

When Congress passed the 1964 Civil Rights Act, it was generally. believed that discrimination took place primarily through conscious, overt actions against individuals. But it quickly became apparent that the processes of discrimination were much more subtle and complex than originally envisioned. It was discovered that normal, seemingly neutral policies such as seniority, aptitude and personnel tests, high school diploma

---

[13] William Henry Chafe, *The American Working Woman: Her Changing Social, Economic and Political Roles, 1920-1970* (1972), p. 188. See also "Women in the Work Force," *E.R.R.*, 1977 Vol. I, pp. 134-135.

[14] See "Negro Jobs and Education," *E.R.R.*, 1963 Vol. I, p. 61.

requirements and college admission tests could perpetuate the effects of past discrimination. This led to the development of the affirmative action concept.

Affirmative Action and Access to Courts

The need for affirmative action was spelled out by President Johnson in a commencement address at Howard University on June 4, 1965.

> Freedom is not enough [Johnson said]. You do not wipe out scars of centuries by saying "now you're free to go where you want and do as you desire." You do not take a person who for years has been hobbled by chains and liberate him, bringing him up to the starting line of a race and then say "you're free to compete" and justly believe that you have been completely fair.

The following Sept. 24 Johnson issued Executive Order 11246 requiring federal contractors "to take affirmative action to ensure applicants are employed, and that employees are treated during employment, without regard to their race, creed, color or national origin."[15] Every major contractor — one having more than 50 employees and a contract of $50,000 or more with the federal government — was required to submit a "written affirmative action compliance program" which would be monitored by the Department of Labor's Office of Federal Contract Compliance.

In January 1970, Secretary of Labor George P. Schultz issued guidelines for the affirmative action plans required by the executive order. The guidelines, which were revised in December 1971, stated that affirmative action was "results oriented." A contractor who was considered to have too few women or minority employees had to establish goals for each job classification, by sex and race, and timetables specifying the date when the situation would be corrected.

Educational institutions originally were not covered by the fair-employment section of the 1964 Civil Rights Act. This oversight was amended by the Equal Employment Opportunity Act of 1972. The act also expanded the powers of the Equal Employment Opportunity Commission. For the first time the commission gained authority to bring civil suits against employers it found to be engaging in discriminatory practices. The act also transferred to the EEOC the Department of Justice's authority to bring suits against a "pattern or practice" of job discrimination.

The 1972 law specified the equal employment responsibilities of the federal government concerning its own personnel. It made

---

[15] Executive Order 11246 was amended in 1967 to apply also to sexual discrimination.

clear that the federal government was required to make all personnel actions free from discrimination on the basis of race, color, religion, sex or national origin; authorized the Civil Service Commission to enforce this policy within the federal bureaucracy; and expressly granted individual federal employees the right to seek relief from such discrimination in the federal courts.[16]

The government's campaign to wipe out employment discrimination has resulted in court decisions and out-of-court settlements costing employers hundreds of millions of dollars in back pay and other benefits. Perhaps the most significant settlements were the two that the EEOC arranged with American Telephone & Telegraph Co. The first, signed in January 1973, applied mostly to women and also to minority-group males who had been denied equal pay and promotion opportunities in non-management jobs. The agency ordered AT&T to award them $15 million in back pay and up to $23 million in pay increases.

The second settlement, filed in May 1974, provided similar awards to management employees who were victims of illegal sex discrimination in pay. "The AT&T decision was important for symbolic reasons...," said Isabel Sawhill, a labor-market economist at the Urban Institute in Washington. "It established that companies have to look at their patterns of employment."[17]

Obstacles to Full Job Equality

PATTERNS of discrimination, in employment and elsewhere, still are evident throughout society. The U.S. Commission on Civil Rights reported in August 1978 that "women and minority men have not achieved equal status with majority males on a series of 21 measures of equality in the areas of education, income, employment, occupations, poverty and housing. Despite some absolute improvement in many of the areas and despite efforts throughout the society to move toward equality ... majority males have continued to enjoy broader opportunities and to reap disproportionate benefits while women and minority males have in many instances fallen even further behind."[18]

---

[16] See Congressional Quarterly, *Congress and the Nation*, Vol. III (1973), pp. 505-509.

[17] Quoted in *Newsweek*, Dec. 16, 1976, p. 69. See also Carol J. Loomis, "AT&T in the Throes of 'Equal Employment,' " *Fortune*, Jan. 15, 1979, p. 45.

[18] U.S. Commission on Civil Rights, "Social Indicators of Equality for Minorities and Women," August 1978, p. 91.

According to the Census Bureau's latest findings, for 1976, average incomes of black and Hispanic families ($9,242 and $10,259, respectively) were approximately two-thirds that of white family income ($15,537). Households headed by white women who worked full-time had incomes less than two-thirds that of white male-headed families. The median income for women in 1976 was $8,312, or only 60 percent of the $13,859 median income for men.[19] One reason for the wage gap between male and female workers and between white and minority workers is that women and minorities continue to be concentrated in the lower-paying job categories. While half of all white men are in professional, managerial or skilled craft occupations, less than one-fourth of the white women and about 30 percent of the minority men and 15 percent of the minority women are so employed.[20]

The wage gap between white and black workers has narrowed in the last three decades, according to reports released by the Rand Corp. in May 1978.[21] In 1947, according to the study, black men earned only half as much as white men; by 1975 that ratio had reached nearly three-quarters. Even greater gains were observed among black women. In 1947 they earned only one-third the wages of white women, but by 1975 their earnings were nearly equal.

Low Level Jobs for Women, Minorities

Increased and improved educational opportunities for blacks and a general improvement in economic conditions in the South were the principal factors behind the wage gains cited in the Rand study. The researchers found that while affirmative action programs had had a positive effect on the wages of black women, they were "a relatively minor contributor to rising relative wages of black men." Affirmative action programs appear to give black women an advantage in the job market. By hiring them, employers can satisfy both minority and female hiring goals.

Evidence of continued disparities in employment opportunities is not limited to the private sector. A report released in December 1977 by the U.S. Commission on Civil Rights noted: "Since 1974, there have been only slight increases in minority and female employment at most levels in the executive branch. Both groups remain heavily concentrated in the lower grades and severely underrepresented in the senior and supergrade

---

[19] U.S. Department of Commerce, Bureau of the Census, "Money Income and Poverty Status of Families and Persons in the United States: 1976," Advance Report, Current Population Reports, series P-60, No. 107, September 1977, table 1.

[20] U.S. Department of Commerce, Bureau of the Census, "Population Profile of the United States: 1976," Current Population Reports, series P-20, No. 307, April 1977, p. 36.

[21] "Race Differences in Earnings: A Survey and New Evidence," Rand Corp., May 1978 and "The Convergence to Racial Equality in Women's Wages," Rand Corp., May 1978.

levels."[22] As of November 1976, the commission said, 17.7 percent of all federal civilian employees were minority group members. This represented an increase of only 0.7 percent since May 1974.

The number of female federal workers increased from 34 percent in 1973 to 35.3 percent in 1975, the latest date for which such statistics are available. Underrepresentation of women and minorities was especially great, the commission said, in levels above grade 15. In 1974 minorities held 3.9 percent of the senior and supergrade positions; by 1976 this figure had risen to only 4.8 percent. According to the commission, women were concentrated in the lowest four grade levels. In 1975 they constituted 76 percent of the employees in those grades.[23] On the other hand, only 2.7 percent of the GS-15 level employees in 1975 were women.

Impact of Preference Laws for Veterans

A serious impediment to recruiting women for upper-level government jobs, the Civil Rights Commission said, is the veterans preference requirement. "Since far more males than females are veterans, this provision . . . has an extremely discriminatory effect upon the employment of women," the commission stated. The U.S. Civil Service Commission estimates that veterans currently account for 50 percent of all federal employees, compared to 22 percent of non-federal workers. Women's rights groups have made the elimination or modification of veterans' preferences one of their top priorities. "This issue is the number one thing affecting the progress of women in government, in hiring and promotions," said Lynn Revo Cohen, chief lobbyist for a coalition of women's and civil rights groups trying to persuade the Carter administration to cut back veterans' preferences.[24]

Under the 1944 Veterans' Preference Act, veterans who were not disabled in service automatically have five points added to their scores on the civil service examinations that determine eligibility for federal jobs. Disabled veterans and their spouses, the mothers of veterans who died in military service and surviving spouses of veterans (as long as they are not remarried) received 10 points. Disabled veterans also are put at the top of lists for those eligible for federal jobs.

The preference points are reusable if a veteran gets one federal job and later decides to compete for another one. A veteran at

---

[22] U.S. Commission on Civil Rights, "The Federal Civil Rights Enforcement Effort - 1977," December 1977, p. 3.

[23] In 1977 the starting salaries for the lowest four grades ranged from $5,810 (GS-1) to $8,316 (GS-4). The starting salary for a GS-15 was $54,410.

[24] Quoted in *The Washington Post*, Feb. 20, 1979.

the top of a Civil Service Commission list of persons competing for a job cannot be passed over by an agency without getting permission from the commission. Veterans also get preference in keeping their jobs if an agency must lay off workers. Some jobs — such as guards, custodians and elevator operators — are reserved solely for veterans eligible for preference.[25]

As part of his plan to overhaul the civil service system, President Carter last year proposed limiting the preference for those veterans who were not disabled to 15 years after leaving the service. In addition, a veteran could only use the preference to get one federal job. He or she then would be protected from layoffs for eight years. Veterans' groups strongly opposed the president's proposals and lobbied actively against them. When the Civil Service Reform bill was approved by Congress last October, the veterans' preference remained intact.

The Carter administration has indicated that it is considering resubmitting its veterans preference proposals. "I think we're likely to try again," Alan Campbell, chairman of the Civil Service Commission, said in an interview last December. "I intend to meet and talk with veterans' groups to see if there's any possibility of compromise."[26] But some White House aides question whether the president will risk antagonizing veterans' groups so close to his expected re-election campaign.

Women's groups are not optimistic that Congress will curtail veterans' preferences. Many see more hope for change in a case now before the U.S. Supreme Court. Helen Feeney, an employee of the state of Massachusetts, was three times denied promotion despite high scores on state civil service examinations, when lower-scoring veterans were placed ahead of her on the state's job eligibility list. Feeney finally sued, charging that the state's preference law discriminated against women. She won in federal district court and last October the Supreme Court agreed to hear the case. A ruling is expected by July 1979.

Future Demographic and Economic Trends

In the future, demographic and economic trends may have as much to do with the progress of the fight against job discrimination as do affirmative action programs. Because of a high population growth rate and the pace of illegal immigration, most analysts predict that Hispanics in the 1980 census will outnumber blacks. This is likely to bring increasing pressure for affirmative action programs geared to the Hispanic community, with a stress on language training. As the influence of brown

---

[25] Veterans' preference does not apply to persons who entered military service after Oct. 14, 1976, and who leave without a disability.

[26] Quoted in *The New York Times*, Dec. 4, 1978.

Americans increases, it is likely that the influence of blacks will diminish. This, in turn, is likely to set off struggles between minority groups over who will wield the most power and influence.

Women outnumber men in terms of total U.S. population and may soon outnumber them in the workplace as well. Over 50 percent of all adult women are in the labor force and women now constitute 41 percent of the nation's workforce. These demographic trends also are likely to have important consequences.[27]

Progress for minorities and women in the past has generally coincided with periods of high economic growth. The civilian economy during World War II was the prime example of this, but the beneficial effects on minorities and women in boom times also was demonstrated during the Vietnam War, when employment soared for all and minorities and women made their greatest gains.

When the economy slows, as was the case in the 1974-75 recession, the old axiom of "last hired, first fired" frequently comes into operation. Affirmative action programs do very little to help people in periods of high unemployment and contracted job markets. The U.S. Civil Rights Commission found that minorities and women are "much more likely than majority men to be unemployed."[28] With many economists predicting slower economic growth for the foreseeable future and the real possibility of a recession in 1979 or 1980, the prospects for substantial progress in eliminating job discrimination, regardless of the fate of legal challenges to affirmative action, seem weak.

---

[27] See "Why Do Women Work, Dear God, Why Do They Work?" *Ms.*, March 1979, pp. 45-46.

[28] "Social Indicators of Equality for Minorites and Women," *op. cit.*, p. 86.

Selected Bibliography

Books

Blaustein, Arthur I. and Geoffrey Faux, *The Star-Spangled Hustle,* Doubleday & Co., 1972.

Hentoff, Nat, *The New Equality,* The Viking Press, 1964.

Jacobson, Julius, ed., *The Negro and the American Labor Movement,* Anchor Books, 1968.

Newman, Dorothy K., et al., *Protest, Politics and Prosperity,* Pantheon Books, 1978.

Jongeward, Dorothy and Dru Scott, *Affirmative Action for Women,* Addison-Wesley Publishing Co., 1975.

Articles

Brown, Gary D., "Discrimination and Pay Disparities Between White Men and Women," *Monthly Labor Review,* March 1978.

Cooper, Ann, "Supreme Court Set to Hear Bias Claim Against Passman," *CQ Weekly Report,* Feb. 17, 1979.

Fortune, selected issues.

Gerard, Paul, "A Tricentennial Portrait," *Civil Rights Digest,* summer 1976.

Kannar, George, "Sears Shall Overcome," *The New Republic,* March 10, 1979.

Leventhal, Harold, "ACES Back to Bakke," *American Bar Association Journal,* February 1979.

Ms., selected issues.

Roberts, Steven V., "The Bakke Case Moves to the Factory," *The New York Times Magazine,* Feb. 25, 1979.

Silver, Isidore, "Death Sentence for Affirmative Action?" *Commonweal,* March 30, 1979.

"The Last Straw," *The Economist,* Feb. 3, 1979.

Reports and Studies

Editorial Research Reports, "Burger Court's Tenth Year," 1978 Vol. II, p. 681; "Negro Employment," 1959 Vol. II, p. 573; "Negroes in the Economy," 1967 Vol. I, p. 181; "Reverse Discrimination," 1976 Vol. II, p. 561; "Women in the Work Force," 1977 Vol. I, p. 121.

General Accounting Office, "The Department of Justice Should Improve Its Equal Employment Opportunity Programs," Feb. 23, 1979; "The Equal Employment Opportunity Commission Has Made Limited Progress in Eliminating Employment Discrimination," Sept. 28, 1976; "Problems in the Federal Employee Equal Employment Opportunity Program Need to Be Resolved," Sept. 9, 1977.

Equal Employment Opportunity Commission, "Legislative History of Titles VII and XI of Civil Rights Act of 1964," August 1968; "Affirmative Action and Equal Employment, A Guidebook for Employers," January 1974.

The Rand Corporation, "Race Differences in Earnings: A Survey and New Evidence," May 1978; "The Convergence to Racial Equality in Women's Wages," May 1978.

U.S. Commission on Civil Rights, "The Federal Civil Rights Enforcement Effort — 1977," December 1977; "Social Indicators of Equality for Minorities and Women," August 1978; "Statement on Affirmative Action," October 1977.

INDEX

A

B

C

R

S

T

U

V

DATE DUE